PRIMATES AND HUMAN ANCESTORS

THE PLIOCENE EPOCH

THE PREHISTORIC EARTH

Early Life:
The Cambrian Period

The First Vertebrates:
Oceans of the Paleozoic Era

March Onto Land:
The Silurian Period to the Middle Triassic Epoch

Dawn of the Dinosaur Age:
The Late Triassic & Early Jurassic Epochs

Time of the Giants:
The Middle & Late Jurassic Epochs

Last of the Dinosaurs:
The Cretaceous Period

The Rise of Mammals:
The Paleocene & Eocene Epochs

The Age of Mammals:
The Oligocene & Miocene Epochs

Primates and Human Ancestors:
The Pliocene Epoch

Early Humans:
The Pleistocene & Holocene Epochs

THE PREHISTORIC EARTH

PRIMATES AND HUMAN ANCESTORS

THE PLIOCENE EPOCH

Thom Holmes

CHELSEA HOUSE
PUBLISHERS
An imprint of Infobase Publishing

THE PREHISTORIC EARTH: Primates and Human Ancestors

Copyright © 2009 by Infobase Publishing

Chelsea House
An imprint of Infobase Publishing
132 West 31st Street
New York NY 10001

Library of Congress Cataloging-in-Publication Data

Holmes, Thom.
   Primates and human ancestors : the pliocene epoch / Thom Holmes.
      p. cm. — (The prehistoric Earth)
   Includes bibliographical references and index.
   ISBN 978-0-8160-5965-2 (hardcover)
  1. Primates, Fossil.   2. Hominids—Evolution.   3. Human evolution.   4. Paleontology—
Pliocene.   I. Title.
   QE882.P7.H65 2008
   569'.8—dc22   2008038328

Text design by Kerry Casey
Cover design by Salvatore Luongo
Section opener images © John Sibbick

Printed in the United States of America

Bang NMSG 10 9 8 7 6 5 4 3 2 1

This book is printed on acid-free paper.

All links and Web addresses were checked and verified to be correct at the time of publication. Because of the dynamic nature of the Web, some addresses and links may have changed since publication and may no longer be valid.

Contents

Preface   6
Acknowledgments   9
Foreword   11
Introduction   13

Section One: Foundations of Human Evolution   17
    Chapter 1 The History of Evolutionary
       Thought   19
    Chapter 2 Mechanisms of Evolution   39
Section Two: Primates   63
    Chapter 3 Origin and Classification of
       the Primates   64
    Chapter 4 Primate Biology and Behavior   82
Section Three: Evolution of the Early Hominins   101
    Chapter 5 The Ape-Hominin Transition   102
    Chapter 6 The Earliest Human Ancestors   121

Conclusion   136
Appendix One: Geologic Time Scale   137
Appendix Two: Anatomical Directions   138
Glossary   139
Chapter Bibliography   143
Further Reading   149
Picture Credits   152
Index   153
About the Author   158

PREFACE

To be curious about the future, one must know something about the past.

Humans have been recording events in the world around them for about 5,300 years. That is how long it has been since the Sumerian people, in a land that is today part of southern Iraq, invented the first known written language. Writing allowed people to document what they saw happening around them. The written word gave a new permanency to life. Language, and writing in particular, made history possible.

History is a marvelous human invention, but how do people know about things that happened before language existed? Or before humans existed? Events that took place before human record keeping began are called *prehistory*. Prehistoric life is, by its definition, any life that existed before human beings existed and were able to record for posterity what was happening in the world around them.

Prehistory is as much a product of the human mind as history. Scientists who specialize in unraveling clues of prehistoric life are called *paleontologists*. They study life that existed before human history, often hundreds of thousands and millions, and even billions, of years in the past. Their primary clues come from fossils of animals, plants, and other organisms, as well as geologic evidence about Earth's topography and climate. Through the skilled and often clever interpretation of fossils, paleontologists are able to reconstruct the appearances, lifestyles, environments, and relationships of ancient life-forms. While paleontology is grounded in a study of prehistoric life, it draws on many other sciences to complete an accurate picture of the past. Information from the fields of biology, zoology, geology, chemistry, meteorology, and even astrophysics is called into play to help the paleontologist view the past through the lens of today's knowledge.

If a writer were to write a history of all sports, would it be enough to write only about table tennis? Certainly not. On the shelves of bookstores and libraries, however, we find just such a slanted perspective toward the story of the dinosaurs. Dinosaurs have captured our imagination at the expense of many other equally fascinating, terrifying, and unusual creatures. Dinosaurs were not alone in the pantheon of prehistoric life, but it is rare to find a book that also mentions the many other kinds of life that came before and after the dinosaurs.

The Prehistoric Earth is a series that explores the evolution of life from its earliest forms 3.5 billion years ago until the emergence of modern humans about 300,000 years ago. Three volumes in the series trace the story of the dinosaurs. Seven other volumes are devoted to the kinds of animals that evolved before, during, and after the reign of the dinosaurs. *The Prehistoric Earth* covers the early explosion of life in the oceans; the invasion of the land by the first land animals; the rise of fishes, amphibians, reptiles, mammals, and birds; and the emergence of modern humans.

The Prehistoric Earth series is written for readers in middle school and high school. Based on the latest scientific findings in paleontology, *The Prehistoric Earth* is the most comprehensive and up-to-date series of its kind for this age group.

The first volume in the series, *Early Life*, offers foundational information about geologic time, Earth science, fossils, the classification of organisms, and evolution. This volume also begins the chronological exploration of fossil life that explodes with the incredible life-forms of Precambrian time and the Cambrian Period, more than 500 million years ago.

The remaining nine volumes in the series can be read chronologically. Each volume covers a specific geologic time period and describes the major forms of life that lived at that time. The books also trace the geologic forces and climate changes that affected the evolution of life through the ages. Readers of *The Prehistoric Earth* will see the whole picture of prehistoric life take shape. They will learn about forces that affect life on Earth, the directions that life can sometimes take, and ways in which all life-forms depend on each other in the environment. Along the way, readers also will meet many of the scientists who have made remarkable discoveries about the prehistoric Earth.

The language of science is used throughout this series, with ample definition and with an extensive glossary provided in each volume. Important concepts involving geology, evolution, and the lives of early animals are presented logically, step by step. Illustrations, photographs, tables, and maps reinforce and enhance the books' presentation of the story of prehistoric life.

While telling the story of prehistoric life, the author hopes that many readers will be sufficiently intrigued to continue studies on their own. For this purpose, throughout each volume, special "Think About It" sidebars offer additional insights or interesting exercises for readers who wish to explore certain topics. Each book in the series also provides a chapter-by-chapter bibliography of books, journals, and Web sites.

Only about one-tenth of 1 percent of all species of prehistoric animals are known from fossils. A multitude of discoveries remain to be made in the field of paleontology. It is with earnest, best wishes that I hope that some of these discoveries will be made by readers inspired by this series.

—Thom Holmes
Jersey City, New Jersey

ACKNOWLEDGMENTS

I want to thank the many dedicated and hardworking people at Chelsea House and Facts on File, some of whom I know but many of whom work behind the scenes. A special debt of gratitude goes to my editors—Frank Darmstadt, Brian Belval, Justine Ciovacco, Shirley White, and Lisa Rand—for their support and guidance in conceiving and making *The Prehistoric Earth* a reality. Frank and Brian were instrumental in fine-tuning the features of the series as well as accepting my ambitious plan for creating a comprehensive reference for students. Brian greatly influenced input during production. Shirley's excellent questions about the science behind the books contributed greatly to the readability of the result. The excellent copyediting of Mary Ellen Kelly was both thoughtful and vital to shaping the final manuscript. I thank Mary Ellen for her patience as well as her valuable review and suggestions that help make the books a success.

The most important collaborators on a series like this are the scientific consultants who lend their time to fact-check and advise the author. I was privileged to work with some of the brightest minds in paleoanthropology on this series. Dr. Conrad Phillip Kottak, professor of anthropology at the University of Michigan, reviewed the draft of *Primates and Human Ancestors* and made many important suggestions that affected the course of the work. Conrad served as the chair of the anthropology department at the University of Michigan from 1996 to 2006, leading one of the most prestigious programs in the country. His work and those of his University of Michigan colleagues, including biologist Richard D. Alexander and paleoanthropologist Milford H. Wolpoff, figure importantly in telling the story of early human evolution. Conrad also wrote the Foreword for the volume.

Breathing life into prehistoric creatures is also the work of natural history artists, many of whom have contributed to this series. I especially want to thank John Sibbick, a major contributor to the artwork seen in *The Prehistoric Earth*. John's work is renowned among paleontologists, many of whom he has worked with side by side.

In many ways, a set of books such as this requires years of preparation. Some of the work is educational, and I owe much gratitude to Dr. Peter Dodson of the University of Pennsylvania for his gracious and inspiring tutelage over the years. I also thank Dr. William B. Gallagher of the New Jersey State Museum for lessons learned in the classroom and in the historic fossil beds of New Jersey. Another dimension of preparation requires experience digging fossils, and for giving me these opportunities I thank my friends and colleagues who have taken me into the field with them, including Phil Currie, Rodolfo Coria, Matthew Lammana, Josh Smith, and Rubén Martínez.

Finally comes the work needed to put thoughts down on paper and complete the draft of a book, a process that always takes many more hours than I plan on. I thank Anne for bearing with my constant state of busy-ness, jokes about jawless fishes, and penguin notes, and for helping me remember the important things in life. You are an inspiration to me. I also thank my daughter, Shaina, the true genius in the family and another constant inspiration, for always being supportive and humoring her father's obsession with prehistoric life, even as he becomes part of it.

FOREWORD

Thom Holmes's series of 10 books, *The Prehistoric Earth,* of which this is Book 9, is written for students. It provides a fascinating and comprehensive introduction to evolutionary thought and theory and to the principles and mechanisms of evolution and genetics developed to explain the origin and diversity of life on Earth, from the earliest organisms to modern humans and our nearest relatives, nonhuman primates.

This volume, *Primates and Human Ancestors,* examines the biology, evolution, and behavior of primates—members of the zoological order that includes ancient and modern humans, apes, monkeys, and lemurs. Continued here is the story of mammal evolution surveyed in the volume *The Age of Mammals.* This book focuses on the primates and the evolutionary developments leading to the rise of hominins—the branch of the primates that includes ancestral and modern humans.

Section One of this volume offers a parsimonious but comprehensive survey of the history of evolutionary thought, along with basic principles and mechanisms responsible for primate and human evolution. Holmes describes the suite of techniques used to reveal evolutionary forces and processes, including applications of genetic research.

Section Two, on nonhuman primates, examines the origin, evolution, and classification of lemurs, monkeys, apes, and humans. Holmes accurately describes the biological and behavioral traits that distinguish primates from other mammalian species.

Section Three focuses on the split between ancestral hominins (our ancestors as distinct from those of chimpanzees and gorillas) and the African apes. Of key importance is the great proliferation of apes during the Miocene Epoch, and the reduction of that variety during the ensuing Pliocene Epoch, in which early hominins abounded. Holmes lays out the defining attributes of early hominins, as well as key differences between them and the apes. This volume concludes with a discussion of variation in time and space among the first undisputed human ancestors.

The story of primate and human origins and evolution is intrinsically fascinating, and Holmes does well to convey the excitement of the field to his intended audience. Remembering my own teen years in public schools, I wish such a series as *The Prehistoric Earth* had existed then. I might have been hooked on a career in paleontology or anthropology even sooner. As it was, I had to wait for college for my introduction to those fields. Knowledge of ape and human evolution has advanced tremendously since those days, and public schools actually have become more tolerant of evolution than when I was in high school. I hope this series and this volume find the large, attentive, and appreciative audience they deserve.

—Conrad Phillip Kottak
University of Michigan

INTRODUCTION

With this volume, *Primates and Human Ancestors*, *The Prehistoric Earth* narrows its evolutionary focus to the lineage of mammals leading to the rise of humans. With this shift, the series steps slightly apart from the examination of general vertebrate paleontology to the specialized study of humans and their ancestors. The field of **anthropology** encompasses the study of human **evolution**, both biological and cultural. **Paleoanthropology**—the study of **fossil** specimens of extinct human ancestors and apes—is the focus of *Primates and Human Ancestors*. The next volume in the series, *Early Humans*, continues the story of human biological evolution while introducing several other specialties in anthropological study, such as the early evolution of language, culture, and societies.

Anthropologist Michael Alan Park of Central Connecticut State University characterizes the field of anthropology as the "holistic study of the human **species**." By *holistic* he means that this is a discipline of research that "assumes an interrelationship among its parts." The biological history of humans is related to the cultural history of humans. The human past is related to the human present.

I am most fortunate to have anthropologist Conrad Kottak (b. 1942) as scientific consultant on this volume. Kottak has taught me that when you begin to look closely into the evolution of humans, you are compelled to look beyond the mere study of fossil bones and teeth to the qualities that make us who we are: a diversity of races, cultures, and beliefs with the will to dream about the future and all of its possibilities. As Kottak has written, "Anthropology is a humanistic science devoted to discovering, describing, and explaining similarities and differences in time and space."

This holistic approach to the study of human evolution has been an underlying goal in the writing of *Primates and Human Ancestors*. Many of the broader issues of human evolution—the development of language, culture, and belief systems—will be fully explored in the *Early Humans* volume of *The Prehistoric Earth*, but the roots of these studies are found in the chapters of this book.

Primates and Human Ancestors continues the story of mammalian evolution that was surveyed in *The Age of Mammals*. This volume concentrates on the primates and on the evolutionary development that led to the rise of **hominins**—the branch of the primates that includes ancestral and modern humans.

OVERVIEW OF *PRIMATES AND HUMAN ANCESTORS*

Primates and Human Ancestors is divided into three sections. Section One, "Foundations of Human Evolution," revisits the science of evolution for the purpose of laying a foundation for the discussion of human origins. Chapter 1 provides a brief history of the figures and social context that were responsible for the development of evolutionary **theory**. The work of Charles Darwin (1809–1882), who publicly proposed his theory of evolution in 1859, is highlighted, and the guiding principles of Darwinism are discussed and brought up to date. The chapter also describes new techniques for exploring and demonstrating the forces of evolution, including the application of genetic research.

Chapter 2, "Mechanisms of Evolution," provides a thorough grounding in the principles that make evolution possible. These include **natural selection** and the influence of both the environment and genetic variation on the development of species.

Section Two, "Primates," begins, in Chapter 3, with an exploration of the origin, evolution, and classification of **Old World** monkeys, **New World** monkeys, and other primates. In Chapter 4, a comparison of primate biology is combined with a discussion of the behavioral traits that make primates unique among mammal species.

Section Three, "Evolution of the Hominins," turns its attention to the rise of human ancestors from the lineage of apes in Africa. In Chapter 5, the similarities between apes and hominins are explored, as are the differences that began to distinguish ancestral humans from apes by the end of the Miocene Epoch. The emergence of the first undisputed human ancestors is discussed in Chapter 6, "The Earliest Human Ancestors." This chapter offers a review of the fossil record of early humans and describes the challenges faced by **paleontologists** and **anthropologists** as they try to trace and understand the lineage of early humans.

As in all volumes of *The Prehistoric Earth*, the discussion in *Primates and Human Ancestors* is governed always by the underlying principles that guide evolution: that the process of evolution is set in motion first by the traits inherited by individuals and then by the interaction of a **population** of a species with those traits with its habitat. As Darwin explained, "The small differences distinguishing varieties of the same species steadily tend to increase, till they equal the greater differences between species of the same **genus**, or even of distinct genera." These are the rules of nature that continually stoke the engine of evolution, giving rise to forms of life whose descendants still populate Earth.

SECTION ONE:
FOUNDATIONS OF
HUMAN EVOLUTION

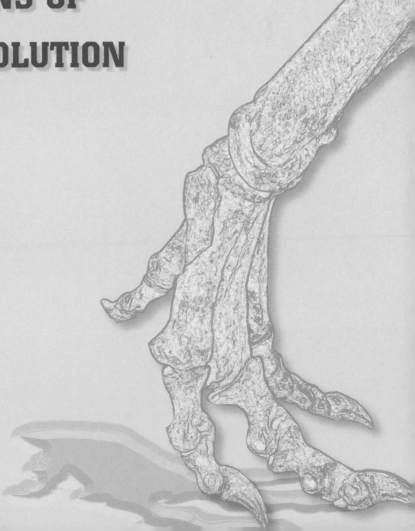

The History of Evolutionary Thought

There are no more profound questions than those about the way in which life evolves. Erwin Schrödinger (1887–1961), a German physicist who was interested in the underlying causes of evolution, fittingly characterized the life of an individual organism as "but a minute blow of the chisel at the ever unfinished statue." Evolution is a work in progress, and the organisms that exist today are only the leading indicators of what will come and what has gone before.

The natural process that causes species to change gradually over time is called *evolution*. This process is driven by changes to the genetic code—the **DNA**—of organisms. These genetic changes are then passed along to the next generation of a species. These changes sometimes result in dramatic changes to a species over many generations and can lead to the rise of new species.

To show the application of evolution to the human species is to show the history of how we descended from nonhuman ancestors and how these changes led to the rise of ***Homo sapiens***—modern humans. This chapter explores the history behind the development of evolutionary theory.

THE PLAYING FIELD OF EARLY EVOLUTIONARY THOUGHT

The study of life origins and the classification of organisms goes back many centuries. As early as the sixth century B.C., the Greek philosopher Anaximander (c. 610–546 B.C.) suggested that the first humans arose from fish and lived a partly aquatic existence until they could fend for themselves on land. Although he did not cite any scientific evidence for his idea, Anaximander used reasoning rather than superstition to explain how humans might have arisen. The Greek philosopher Aristotle (384–322 B.C.) was one of the first scientific thinkers to attempt a classification of life. He divided organisms into the two kingdoms of plants and animals. Aristotle's two kingdoms stood the test of time for several centuries.

Early evolutionary ideas were not exclusively Western. The Chinese philosopher Zhuangzi (c. 370–301 B.C.), sometimes known as Chuang Tsu, was the purported author and editor of a seminal collection of works related to the philosophy of Taoism. In these writings, the author touched on the ability of living things to adapt and transform in response to their surroundings, a process that often went unnoticed and that affected humans as well as other living things.

The Persian philosopher-scientist Ibn Miskawayh (932–1030) described the progressive development of life through a series of stages that began with God's creation of matter and energy. From matter came air and water, minerals, plants, and finally apes and humans. Miskawayh's description of linked but increasingly sophisticated stages of development of matter and organisms strongly hinted at undefined processes such as those involved in natural selection.

The European Taxonomists

The European road to a scientific theory of evolution had its beginnings in the seventeenth and eighteenth centuries. The building of the road began with the work of natural scientists and their efforts to categorize and describe living plants and animals—the practice of **taxonomy**. British naturalist John Ray (1627–1705) was a botanist who used observation to classify plants and animals according to similarities in their biological structures. He also was the first scientist to use the terms *genus* and *species* to classify different plants and animals.

Ray was followed by the great Swedish botanist Carolus Linnaeus (1707–1778), who introduced an intricate new methodology for grouping and naming organisms within the two kingdoms of plants and animals. With the publication of his groundbreaking work *Systema Naturae* in 1758, Linnaeus suggested that nature could be further organized into a grand hierarchy of groups within groups. Linnaeus recognized a species as the most basic biological unit of life, and he grouped species within ever-widening categories of organisms based on the similarities of their visible structures. Dogs, for example, are part of a group, the carnivora, or **carnivorous** (meat-eating) animals, that also includes such diverse animals as cats, bears, pandas, weasels, sea lions, and walruses, among others. The carnivora, in turn, are part of a larger group, the mammals. Mammals, in their turn, are grouped in yet a larger group with other animals with backbones: the vertebrates. This larger group includes fish, amphibians, reptiles, and birds. The vertebrates are then grouped with all animals without backbones to form the kingdom of animals. This nested hierarchy of groups was widely accepted and refined for more than 200 years, until genetic studies provided a more accurate method of determining the evolutionary relationships of organisms.

In choosing the species as his basic building block for classification, Linnaeus also was the first scientist to establish a rule that reflected a fundamental mechanism behind evolution: Traits are passed on from one generation to the next through genetic material. Although Linnaeus and other scientists of the eighteenth and nineteenth centuries had no direct evidence of **genes**, DNA, or the way in which traits are passed from one generation to the next, these scientists were able to establish rules behind evolution that were observable in living organisms.

The European Geologists

Another road to evolutionary thought in Europe was paved by the work of geologists working in the eighteenth and nineteenth centuries. At issue was the age of the Earth. Linnaeus, Ray, and other

European scientists were greatly influenced by religious beliefs that originated with the biblical stories of creation, the Garden of Eden, the Great Flood, and Noah's ark. In the seventeenth and eighteenth centuries, most philosophers and scientists agreed with a literal interpretation of the Bible: God created the universe in six days, and all known creatures were created by God at the same time. The very concept of **extinction**—the idea that no species lasts forever—was unacceptable because it implied that life was somehow imperfect, that species came and went, and that one day people, as a species, would also perish from the Earth. It was not generally recognized that many forms of life had existed before the time of the first humans. One Irish archbishop, James Ussher (1581–1656), even used the written account of the Bible to calculate the precise date of the creation of the Earth. He proclaimed that it all began at noon on Sunday, October 23, 4004 B.C., thus making Earth about 6,000 years old.

During the seventeenth century, natural scientists began to recognize fossils as evidence of past life. Fossils strongly suggested that some species of organisms had become extinct. This observation naturally led to a discussion of the age of such fossils and to a growing conflict between religious interpretations of the age of the Earth and observations made in the natural world.

The key to the age of the Earth was to be found in **sedimentary** rocks. Naturalists observed that such rocks accumulated in layers, with the oldest on the bottom. The telltale signs of passing time were recorded in these layers of rocks because all of these rock layers had accumulated over time by means of the same processes.

Scottish geologist James Hutton (1726–1797) proposed a natural cycle by which Earth replenishes itself. Hutton theorized that rocks eroded from mountains were transported by rivers and streams to the ocean. In the ocean, these rocks sank as deposits to the bottom, where subterranean forces of heat and gravitational pressure turned the fragmentary deposits into solid rocks once again. The action of earthquakes and volcanoes might one day raise these newly formed rocks to the surface again, to gradually form new mountains and other land forms. The most startling aspect of Hutton's theory was

Scottish geologist James Hutton (1726–1797) proposed a natural cycle by which the Earth replenishes itself.

that he estimated the time needed to accommodate this cycle as enormously long—much longer than human history or any time scale in use in the eighteenth century.

Hutton published his innovative ideas in 1785 in a book called *Theory of the Earth*. His idea that the age of the Earth could be determined by observing present-day geologic processes was called *uniformitarianism.* Hutton is called the father of geology by many historians, and he can be credited with laying the foundation for modern geology.

Around the time of Hutton's death in 1797, a young British surveyor and mapmaker named William Smith (1769–1839) observed that the rocks into which mine shafts had been drilled contained a regular and predictable pattern of stratigraphic rock layers, or *strata.* Because these strata could be seen in widespread locations, this suggested a regularity to geologic formations. Furthermore, certain strata contained the same fossils, no matter where an outcropping of a given layer might lay. Smith was not a man of science, but his detailed stratigraphic maps of the area surrounding the city of Bath (1799) and all of England (1815) were the first credible geologic maps.

British naturalist Sir Charles Lyell (1797–1875) was born the same year that James Hutton died. To introduce Hutton's ideas to a wider audience became Lyell's passion. He traveled widely in search of evidence to prove that Hutton was correct, and he armed himself with compelling findings.

Lyell embraced Hutton's theory of uniformitarianism. In 1830, Lyell distilled this complex theory down to a simple guiding principle to explain the age of the Earth: *The present is the key to the past.* Lyell's momentous book, *Principles of Geology,* became the bible of geology and was revised 12 times in Lyell's lifetime.

Lyell's seemingly commonsense proposition—that observing the present is the key to understanding how geologic features were created over time—was a bold realization in his day. Given enough time to work, natural forces slowly and dramatically change the face of the Earth. The time that it takes today for layers of the Earth to accumulate through erosion, water transport, drought, and other forces is the same time that it took in the past. This is an exceedingly slow process by human time standards, but it accounts for the great age of the Earth. These actions might take thousands, perhaps even millions, of years. Such an idea seemed impossible

British naturalist Sir Charles Lyell (1797–1875) provided a simple guiding principle to explain the age of the Earth: The present is the key to the past.

to people who believed that Earth was only 6,000 years old. Soon, however, many natural scientists and geologists began to support the principle of uniformitarianism through the proof of their own observations.

Communicating the length of time needed to explain the process of Earth's geologic features required geologists to develop a new scale for measuring time. The result was a time scale based on the layers of the Earth and how long these layers took to accumulate. This scale is called the geologic time scale. Because no given species of plant or animal exists forever, the fossil remains of a given species are restricted to certain layers.

By the middle nineteenth century, there was widespread agreement that Earth was many millions of years old. Just how many millions of years was still a matter of debate, however. By 1860, the prevailing view, supported by Lyell, was that Earth was a minimum of 200 million years old and perhaps as many as 340 million years old. The measurement of the age of the Earth was further refined by the discovery, in 1895, of radioactivity. An understanding of radioactive isotopes and the rate at which they decay over many millions of years made it possible to date many layers of the Earth, with little doubt, to within years. The current calculation that Earth is 4.5 billion years old was arrived at around 1953.

Early efforts to classify organisms by their shared, observable traits and an understanding of the natural geologic forces that shape the Earth provided a foundation on which the theory of evolution could be developed.

A HISTORY OF EVOLUTIONARY THEORY

The individual who is most closely associated with the theory of evolution is British naturalist Charles Darwin. As in most major scientific endeavors, breakthroughs in evolutionary thought were achieved in small steps and by many people, some working before, some during, and some after the time of Darwin. Darwin is so closely associated with evolution because he was perhaps more successful than his contemporaries in illustrating and explaining the processes of evolution in a way that most people could understand.

Before an exploration of the origins of modern evolutionary thought, a word about theories is in order. In everyday conversation, the term *theory* can have many meanings. Usually, it signifies merely a conjecture, an idea, or an opinion. A conjecture does not have to be based on facts, and it does not require proof. One might

British naturalist Charles Darwin (1809–1882), the father of modern
evolutionary thought

theorize, for example, that a student who comes to school one day dressed more formally than usual might be attending an important occasion later that same day.

In science, the term *theory* has the opposite meaning. A scientific theory is not based on mere conjecture. A scientific theory is, instead, a comprehensive explanation of some aspect of the natural world that is backed by an extensive body of facts built up over time. A scientific theory is testable and can be used to accurately predict future, yet-unobserved events and phenomena.

Evolution is a scientific theory, backed by an extensive history of facts. Evolution is not a matter of conjecture, although it is often portrayed as such by opponents of evolution who are not well versed in science or who choose to distort the concept of evolution for their own social, religious, or political purposes. This is not to suggest that religious beliefs and the theory of evolution cannot coexist peaceably. They do coexist, quite harmoniously, in the minds of most religious leaders and scientists. A belief in God does not preclude a belief in evolution.

When viewed as a scientific theory, evolution has a rich history of discovery and proof, much of which revolved originally around the life and times of Darwin, evolution's most eloquent advocate.

Darwin was a reader of Lyell, and he understood uniformitarianism: The present is the key to the past. Not only did Lyell's work provide an appropriately long time for the mechanisms of evolution to take place, but it also inspired Darwin to sharpen his own observation of the present as a window on the past.

Another influence on Darwin was his grandfather, Erasmus Darwin (1731–1802). Erasmus was a physician and a celebrity in the literary circles of his day. Among Erasmus Darwin's numerous writings and letters, many of which his grandson Charles is known to have read, were speculations on evolutionary concepts. In a book of verse called *Zoonomia*, published in 1794, Erasmus Darwin wrote that "organic life began beneath the waves," thus suggesting that all animal species had a common ancestry in the oceans.

Before the term *evolution* was widely used, the process of evolution was known by a variety of other names. Most of these names referred back to the observable changes that can be seen in a species from generation to generation. Terms such as *transformism* and *the transmutation of species* or *the transformation of species* often were used to describe this process for which the underlying mechanisms were not yet fully understood.

One of the first scientists who tried to explain the transformation of species was Jean-Baptiste Lamarck (1744–1829), an accomplished French scholar. Writing long before Charles Darwin, Lamarck believed there was a dynamic connection between the development of living organisms and their environment. Lamarck thought that an organism could be altered by circumstantial changes in the environment, and that such alterations could be passed along to offspring. Lamarck's most often cited example was that of the neck of the giraffe. According to Lamarck, giraffes were descended from short-necked ancestors. These ancestors stretched and stretched to reach higher and higher branches on trees. Because of the stretching, the neck of the ancestral giraffe became slightly longer, and the length of the neck was passed along to the next generation. Descendants with longer and longer necks developed after many generations of giraffes.

Larmarckism became known as the **theory of acquired characteristics**. According to this theory, it was through the interaction of successive generations of a species with the environment that new species developed. Variation in a species occurred more or less by necessity. Whereas Lamarck is credited with recognizing the important relationship between a species and the environment, his theory did not take into consideration what we now understand to be the genetic foundation of evolution. Lamarck offered no mechanism behind the acquisition of traits other than the "will" or need to make it so on the part of the organism. His theory met with serious objections based on some easily observable exceptions. If, for example, instead of a long neck, one considered an acquired characteristic such as the accidental loss of an arm or a scar on the face, why were these traits not passed along to offspring? How could the "will" of an organism distinguish between such acquired traits so as to pass some along and not others?

Charles Darwin

Charles Darwin was born into a large, wealthy family and raised in the English countryside. He spent his youth enjoying the outdoors, fishing and hunting and becoming a keen observer of nature. He was sent to college to study medicine and theology but also was keen on the study of geology and Lyell's theories.

Darwin's world was one in which it was generally accepted that the biological nature of species changed over time but that no scientific mechanism was yet known to explain how this happened. The prevailing theory about **speciation** was that of Lamarck. Darwin doubted Lamarckism for a very simple reason: One could observe more variation in living species than could be explained by Lamarck's theory of acquired traits. If Lamarck's theory were true, one would expect species exposed to the same environmental conditions all to be about the same. This clearly was not true, however. Darwin's own experience raising domestic pigeons told him that one could selectively breed in and breed out certain desired or undesired traits that were passed along to the next generation despite the fact that all of the birds were exposed to the same environment. Thus began Darwin's quest for a theory that would explain how this happened.

Another important influence on Darwin was the British political economist Thomas Malthus (1766–1834), whose *Essay on the Principle of Population* was published in 1798. One of the themes of Malthus' work was the relationship between population growth and competition for material resources to maintain such a population. Malthus showed that population growth outpaced the ability of resource production to keep pace with it, resulting in such problems as malnutrition, famine, and social unrest. The underlying concept suggested by Malthus was that competition was inevitable, an idea that impressed Darwin and that would later become an important element in his own theories.

At age 22, after graduating from Cambridge University, Darwin joined a scientific expedition. That expedition circled the globe on a five-year voyage and provided astonishing opportunities for the young naturalist. During the voyage of HMS *Beagle* from 1831 to 1836, Darwin was immersed in geological work and the description of animal species that the expedition encountered. His discovery of fossils of creatures that shared traits with living forms gave him reason to believe that modern animals were descended from long-extinct ancestors.

Of most relevance to Darwin's emerging ideas about species were observations made on the Galápagos Islands, off the coast of Ecuador. Darwin noticed that each island in the system had many of the same species of animals, but with significant variations from island to island. The traits of Galápagos finches were of particular interest. Although it appeared that the island finches were descended from finches on the mainland, each island produced finches with differences in particular physical traits, primarily the shape and size of the beak. Each group of island finches was adapted for a particular kind of food that was most prevalent on a particular island: a heavy beak for crunching big seeds; a thick, short beak for eating leaves, buds, and fruits; or a straight, pointed beak for picking insects from tree bark.

Darwin's theories were based on two important observations. He could see that offspring inherit physical traits from their parents. Furthermore, he could see that offspring are never identical to their parents, and that no two offspring of the same parents are identical. Each offspring includes a unique combination of characteristics inherited from its parents.

Darwin also observed that many more offspring are produced by a species than will survive long enough to reproduce on their own. From these observations, Darwin drew two significant conclusions. The first was that in our world of many diverse living things, there is an ongoing struggle for survival. Adapting the ideas of Malthus, Darwin wrote that "many more individuals of each species are born than can survive." He saw that the variation of traits within a given species makes some individuals more likely to survive. The reasons why some individuals survive and others do not led Darwin to his second conclusion: Given the complex and changing conditions under which life exists, those individuals with the most favorable combination of inherited traits may survive and reproduce while other individuals may not. Nature is the judge and jury of which individuals make the grade. For this reason, Darwin called this process *natural selection*, meaning that the natural laws of inheritance provided or assured, by chance, some members of a species to be better equipped for survival than others.

On his return to England, Darwin meticulously documented his theory of natural selection and continued to make observations. He shared his ideas with colleagues but was slow to publish his views. He drafted short sketches about natural selection in 1842 and 1844, but he felt the need to continue his research and document evidence before he was ready to formerly publish his views for the world.

Darwin was not alone in this quest. Alfred Russel Wallace (1823–1913) was another British naturalist, working independently of Darwin. While on his own travels, Wallace studied and collected specimens of plants, insects, and birds, much as Darwin did. Wallace also arrived at some of the same conclusions as Darwin.

Wallace published a paper in 1855 suggesting that the development of new species was driven by environmental forces. Even more startling to Darwin was a paper Wallace sent to him in 1858, in which the younger naturalist described the process of natural selection. Darwin's heart sank. Although not normally a competitive man, Darwin indeed feared that Wallace might receive full credit for the theory of "natural selection" that he himself had been working on for nearly 30 years. In response, Darwin dashed off a paper about his own theories.

The papers by Darwin and Wallace were read at the same meeting of London's Linnaean Society in 1858. After that, Darwin's wife, along with Charles Lyell and others, urged Darwin to follow up with a more thorough explanation of his theory. The result was Darwin's seminal book, *On the Origin of Species by Means of Natural Selection*, published at the end of 1859. Although Wallace is duly credited with having also developed the theory of evolution by natural selection, the spotlight landed on Darwin because of his success at communicating the theory beyond the scientific community.

Darwin's views were not universally accepted in his time. Even though his observations were astute and his deductions convincing, Darwin was constrained, as were all nineteenth-century scientists, by a lack of knowledge regarding genetics, the underlying biological mechanism behind evolution. Chapter 2 introduces the biological principles that govern evolution and make it possible.

THE GUIDING PRINCIPLES OF DARWINISM

The evolutionary principles laid out by Darwin, often referred to as Darwinism, have remained the foundation of evolutionary study and debate since his time. Darwin's view of evolution was built on five basic rules and assumptions. Ernst Mayr (1904–2005), a leading twentieth-century evolutionary biologist who was instrumental in modernizing evolutionary study, interpreted Darwin's principles in the following way:

Species change over time; they are not constant. Darwin's own work provided evidence in support of this tenet. Mayr further clarified the meaning of "species" by showing, in 1942, that a species was not merely a group of **morphologically** similar individuals, but a group of individuals that could breed only among themselves, to the exclusion of other species.

All organisms arose from a common ancestral population. Although this statement was controversial at first, Darwin provided information to show that this was indeed the case, based on evidence that could be seen in the present.

Evolutionary modifications occur gradually. Although it is widely accepted that evolution requires a long span of time and many generations of a species to manifest the generation of new species

THINK ABOUT IT

TIMELINE OF EARLY EVOLUTION THOUGHT

Person	Year	Contribution
Anaximander (c. 610–546 B.C.)	c. 600 B.C.	Suggested that the ancestors of humans were fish.
Aristotle (384–322 B.C.)	c. 350 B.C.	Divided organisms into the two kingdoms of plants and animals.
Zhuangzi (c. 370–301 B.C.)	c. 330 B.C.	Suggested that organisms can change (adapt) in response to their environment.
Ibn Miskawayh (932–1030)	c. 1000	Described the progressive development of life through natural processes.
James Ussher (1581–1656)	1650	Used biblical data to calculate the age of the Earth.
John Ray (1627–1705)	1686	Used the terms *genus* and *species* to classify different plants and animals.
Carolus Linnaeus (1707–1778)	1735–1779	Defined a sophisticated method of classifying plants and animals.
Comte Georges-Louis Leclerc de Buffon (1707–1788)	1749	Recognized that the environment could cause change in a species; suggested a longer age for the Earth.
James Hutton (1726–1797)	1785	Showed that the age of the Earth could be determined by observing present-day geologic processes; his theory, called *uniformitarianism*, suggested a longer age for the Earth.
Charles Lyell (1797–1875)	1830	Defined the guiding principle to explain the age of the Earth: *The present is the key to the past.*
Erasmus Darwin (1731–1802)	1794	Published *Zoonomia*, suggesting that all animal species had a common ancestry.
Jean-Baptiste Lamarck (1744–1829)		Linked environment to species change; developed the theory of acquired characteristics.
Charles Darwin (1809–1882)	1859	Published *On the Origin of Species by Means of Natural Selection*.
Alfred Wallace (1823–1913)	1859	Published his views on natural selection.

from old, there is continuing debate, even today, as to the pace of evolution. Although Darwin was satisfied to demonstrate that the evolution of present-day species was preceded by millions of years of development and natural selection, it appears that the rate of evolution might vary, from a state of extreme **gradualism** to one of accelerated change based on the environmental circumstances faced by a species. The rate of evolutionary change is explored in Chapter 2.

A single species can diversify into more than one species. While the development of new species from old—speciation—is widely accepted, the mechanisms that make this possible are the source of continuing study and debate. Issues related to speciation are discussed in Chapter 2.

Natural selection is the primary process of evolution. Although accepted on principle during Darwin's lifetime, the genetic mechanism that made natural selection possible was not discovered until more than 50 years after his death. Ernst Mayr worked during the era in which the mechanisms of biological molecules, genes, and DNA were discovered. He never fully embraced molecular evolutionary studies that placed an emphasis on the influence of individual genes over all other environmental pressures on a species, however. Mayr argued that evolutionary pressures affected the whole organism, not only single genes, and that the influence of individual genes also depended on the collective effect of other genes that were present. Current understanding of natural selection is more thoroughly explored in Chapter 2.

CONCLUSION

Charles Darwin succeeded in presenting a foundation for evolutionary theory that has stood the test of time and now is documented by countless observations and experiments. In Darwin's own lifetime, however, his ideas were not widely accepted at first. Opposed to Darwin's theory was a well-established school of thought characterized by Lamarck's theory of the inheritance of acquired characteristics—the idea that the interaction of an individual with the environment could result in biological changes that could be passed on to offspring. By providing a logical alternative to the inheritance of acquired characteristics, Darwin's theory of natural selection did much to dispel Lamarck's theory. The difference between Lamarck's theory and Darwin's can be shown by returning to the story of Lamarck and his giraffes.

According to Lamarck, giraffes attained their long necks gradually, by acquiring slight increases in height, generation after generation, as the animals stretched to reach tree foliage that grew higher and higher above their reach. For this process to work, each individual giraffe in each generation would have had to encounter the same environmental problem—ever-taller trees—and would have had to stretch with equal intent to effect a slight increase in the length of its neck and legs. These slight increases were then passed along to each individual giraffe's offspring, causing each generation to grow slightly taller. Lamarck's explanation relied on environmental conditions remaining constant for each generation of giraffes and assumed that the giraffes themselves would exercise the "will" to stretch themselves to reach higher branches.

In contrast, Darwin (and Wallace) believed that the process of natural selection could account for the evolution of height in giraffes. According to natural selection, variation has always existed in the length of giraffe necks. In cases in which having a longer neck provided an advantage for feeding, giraffes with longer necks that benefited from this advantage would have been more likely to pass this trait along to their offspring than less advantaged giraffes. Over many generations, the trait of longer and longer necks gradually would have prevailed, even though variation in neck length still exists among the entire population of giraffes.

In time, the preponderance of scientific evidence clearly supported Darwin's view over that of Lamarck and established evolution by means of natural selection as the foundation of modern biological sciences.

Living species represent moments in the ongoing process of evolution. There is no such thing as a species that has stopped evolving. Humans and all other species on the planet continue to change with each successive generation, even if only in ways that are nearly imperceptible. Evolution is influenced by inherited traits and by changes in the environment. Knowing how these kinds of changes affected past organisms is a key to seeing the future of life.

To know the past is to understand the present.

SUMMARY

This chapter has reviewed the historical background and key contributors to the development of evolutionary thought.

1. The study of the origins of life and the classification of organisms goes back many centuries.

2. The taxonomic work of John Ray and Carolus Linnaeus established a means for recognizing classifications of plants and animals based on their observable, physical structures.

3. Scottish geologist James Hutton proposed a natural cycle by which Earth replenishes itself. He established the idea of uniformitarianism: that the age of the Earth could be determined by observing present-day geologic processes In doing this, Hutton proved that Earth was much older than previously had been believed.

4. Charles Lyell, expanding on Hutton's work, established a guiding principle to explain the age of the Earth: *The present is the key to the past.*

5. The individual who is most closely associated with the theory of evolution is British naturalist Charles Darwin.

6. A scientific theory is a statement of fact that is testable and can be used to accurately predict future, yet-unobserved events and phenomena. Evolution is a scientific theory, backed by an extensive history of facts.

7. One of the first scientists to try to explain the transformation of species was Jean-Baptiste Lamarck, best known for his theory of acquired characteristics.

8. Charles Darwin and Alfred Russel Wallace both published their findings regarding natural selection in 1858.

9. Darwin published his book *On the Origin of Species by Means of Natural Selection* in 1859, and it became the foundation of evolutionary science.

10. Ernst Mayr wrote in 1942 that species were not merely a group of morphologically similar individuals, but a group of individuals that could breed only among themselves, to the exclusion of other species. This definition effectively modernized Darwin's theory by introducing genetics as the underlying mechanism that makes speciation possible.

MECHANISMS OF EVOLUTION

Charles Darwin understood that for natural selection to function, there had to be variation within the species population in question. Although Darwin could observe the results of natural selection by studying variation in plants and animals, he was unaware of the mechanism that made this process possible. The science of genetics, which emerged after the time of Darwin, provides the biochemical basis for the inheritance of traits that results in variation within a species. Thus, evolution is based on two factors: variation within a species and natural selection that acts on individuals within a population. In operating on individuals, natural selection affects the survival and opportunity of those individuals to reproduce, thereby allowing traits to be passed on to offspring. Offspring are subject to natural selection as well. Over time, the evolution of populations— and in due course, species—is effected.

This chapter examines the fundamentals of genetics and the natural forces that cause evolutionary change.

THE DISCOVERY OF INHERITANCE PATTERNS

Although Darwin's remarkable synthesis of observations and deduction allowed him to posit the existence of natural selection as a verifiable force in the evolution of species, he was without knowledge of the underlying biological mechanisms that made natural selection possible. He admitted as much in 1859, writing in *On the Origin of Species*, "The laws governing inheritance are for the most part unknown. No one can say why the same peculiarity in different individuals of the same species, or in different species, is sometimes inherited and sometimes not so." Darwin was unable to explain how traits were passed on.

Gregor Mendel (1822–1884) was an Austrian monk, unknown to Darwin, whose experiments raising peas in a garden provided some answers to the puzzle of inheritance. Mendel worked in relative obscurity for many years, and he, like Darwin, had no knowledge about the biochemical basis of inheritance. Nevertheless, Mendel's groundbreaking work laid the foundation for the science of genetics.

Mendel was fascinated with the variety of traits exhibited by a common variety of pea plant. These traits varied when the plants were bred, and Mendel wondered whether there was a practicable pattern operating that managed the appearance of such traits as plant height, the arrangement of flowers on the branch, and the color of the pea pods. Mendel's curiosity, his keen observational skills, and his zeal for record keeping drove him to experiment with thousands of plants, for which he carefully recorded cross-pollination combinations and results. The patterns that he discovered are now known as Mendelian genetics and provided the first basic understanding of inheritance patterns and the general laws governing genetic code.

In 1856, working primarily with pea plants, Mendel began eight years of extensive breeding experiments. Pollinating the plants by hand, he crossed plants that exhibited any one of seven obvious traits and duly recorded the traits of their offspring. The plant traits were easy to identify and included such factors as smooth or wrinkled seeds, tall or short stems, and green or yellow pods. Mendel's experiments were the first systematic study of inheritance patterns. His work encompassed so many examples that reliably predictable patterns began to appear.

Prior to Mendel's work, scientists had only the fuzziest understanding of inheritance. Most scholars still held to Lamarck's principle of acquired characteristics—that a physical change acquired in life could be passed along to an offspring. It also was believed that

Gregor Mendel (1822–1884) was an Austrian monk whose experiments raising peas in a garden provided some answers to the puzzle of inheritance.

offspring contained an intermediate blend of all the traits found in the parents. Once passed on to an offspring, the fullness of a parent's trait was lost forever.

In one series of experiments, Mendel combined tall and short plants and produced only tall offspring. By repeatedly breeding the offspring of these tall plants, however, Mendel showed that short plants began to reappear in successive generations. Among the thousands of results in this sequence of breedings, a ratio of one short plant to every three tall plants emerged.

Mendel discovered that inheritance did not occur through a blending, or lessening, of traits from both parents, but through a combination of discrete units that he called "particulate factors" and that now are called genes. Genes represent traits that can disappear in one generation but reappear in a later generation in their original form. Mendel correctly surmised that two genes are required for each trait. Among Mendel's discoveries were the following:

Inheritance of each trait in an offspring is determined by discrete "particulate factors" (now called genes). These traits are passed along to the offspring unchanged.

The offspring possesses two genes for each trait—one from each parent. These genes may come in versions that are different, called alleles.

Gene expression is governed by three possible combinations of alleles for each trait. An offspring acquires one gene from each parent. These genes may come in different versions, making three possible combinations in the resulting genes of the offspring. These combinations are called genotypes. Having two of the same alleles for a given gene is a condition known as being homozygous. Having a pair of nonmatching alleles for a gene is a condition known as being heterozygous.

The genotype determines which trait will be expressed. The observable trait itself, such as the color of a person's eyes, is known as the phenotype.

Some alleles will be expressed over other alleles. In a heterozygous combination, one of the alleles must be expressed; that allele is known as the dominant allele. The allele that is masked by the dominant allele is called the recessive allele. A recessive allele, or trait, is not destroyed and may be expressed in a later generation.

Trait exhibited by F$_1$ hybrids	F$_2$ generation (produced by crossbreeding F$_1$ hybrids)	
	Exhibit dominant trait	Exhibit recessive trait
Smooth seed shape	Smooth 3	Wrinkled 1
Yellow seed interior	Yellow 3	Green 1
Gray seed coat	Gray 3	White 1
Inflated pod	Inflated 3	Pinched 1
Green pod	Green 3	Yellow 1
Axial pod	Axial 3	Terminal 1
Tall stem	Tall 3	Short 1
	Offspring exhibit dominant or recessive traits in ratio of 3:1	

Mendel's experiments with pea plants revealed the basic patterns of inheritance.

Traits can be inherited independently of one another. The expression of one gene is not dependent on the expression of other genes. All possible combinations of traits are possible, thus providing great variety in a population. The recombination of traits is vital to the biology of evolution because it creates a variety of traits on which natural selection operates.

Mendel published the results of his plant hybridization experiments in 1866, in the scientific proceedings of the Natural History Society of Brünn, in Germany. His landmark findings failed to gain wide notice or acceptance until after his death, however.

THE BIOCHEMICAL BASIS FOR INHERITED TRAITS

Mendel's experiments clearly demonstrated that a biochemical basis for his "particulate factors" probably existed. By the end of the nineteenth century, it was postulated that living organisms possessed a biochemical blueprint within living cells that was responsible for transmitting traits from parents to offspring. Continued advances in biochemistry progressively led to an understanding of chromosomes, genes, and finally DNA—the double-stranded molecule, found in every cell, that is the carrier of genetic material. All of these elements may be classed as being genetic material, intimately involved in the body's machinery of inheritance.

By definition, there are several required functions of genetic material:

- Genetic material must contain all of the instructions needed to construct an entire organism. The complete instructions are called the **genome** of an organism.
- It must be possible for genetic material to be passed from parent to offspring and then from cell to cell during the process of cell division.
- It must be possible to accurately duplicate genetic material for that genetic material to make exact copies of itself. This is

the feature that makes it possible to transmit genetic material from parent to offspring.

- Variation found in genetic material will represent the entire range of possible variation within a species.

The purpose of genetic code is to provide instructions for the construction of cells. This is done through the chemical synthesis of *proteins* from *amino acids*. Amino acids are found in the food that we eat and are contained in the cytoplasm—the gelatinous fluid that makes up much of the volume of each cell in an organism. Of the 20 amino acids found in human cells, 11 are synthesized by the cells themselves, but nine, known as essential amino acids, can be obtained only from the food that we eat.

Proteins are organic compounds made from amino acids. Proteins are literally the building blocks of cells. Proteins provide structure and create an environment for other chemical processes to occur. Proteins are also used to build connective tissue, membranes, and muscle in the body. Proteins known as *enzymes* are specialized to produce chemical reactions involved with such widely different functions as digestion, muscle contraction, and the transmission of signals from cell to cell.

DNA—short for deoxyribonucleic acid—is the molecule that carries genetic code. Genes are located on strands of DNA. The structure of DNA is like two strands of string twisted around each other and is also called a double helix. The two strands in the double helix are connected by steps like those in a ladder. The biochemical makeup of DNA specifies the order in which amino acids are arranged during protein synthesis. The biochemical structure and components of DNA also make it possible for genes to replicate and make copies of themselves—one of the primary functions of genetic materials that allows traits to be passed along to offspring.

A gene is the smallest hereditary unit. Genes are bundled onto DNA. The next largest genetic unit is the chromosome, comprising both DNA (containing associated genes) and protein.

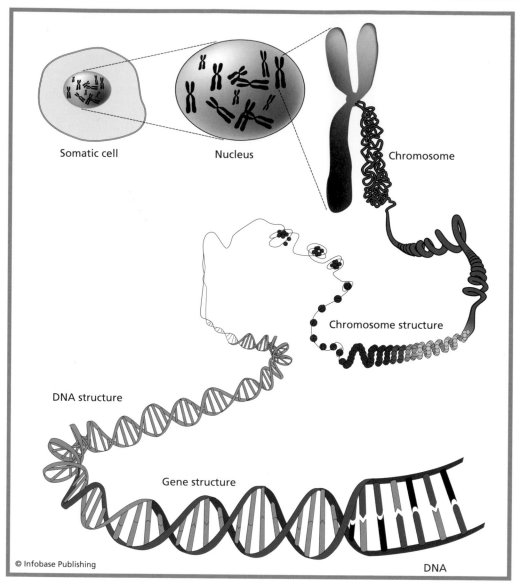

© Infobase Publishing

Chromosome structure and DNA

The cells of the body, except those involved in reproduction, are called *somatic* cells. Every somatic cell in an organism has the same number of chromosomes. Humans have 23 different chromosomes, each of which can have from 300 to 2,000 genes. In addition, humans and most other organisms have two copies of each chromosome in each cell—one copy from the mother and one from the father. Humans, therefore, have a total of 46 chromosomes in their somatic cells.

Cells involved in sexual reproduction are called gametes and contain only half of the chromosomes—23 in the case of humans. For the purpose of reproducing, a gamete will join with another sex cell, also containing 23 chromosomes, and the combination will provide the full complement of 46 chromosomes required by the human cell. When two organisms mate, the resulting offspring contains a unique combination of genes derived from the parents' DNA.

THE EVOLUTION OF INDIVIDUALS AND POPULATIONS

The science of genetics was first observed by Gregor Mendel and then articulated at the biochemical level through the discovery and study of genes and DNA. The genetic process begins at the level of the individual and the inheritance of traits from parents to offspring.

Evolution begins with a population of individuals in which breeding is possible. **Population genetics** is the study of the frequency of alleles, genotypes, and phenotypes in a given group of individuals. The combined genetic makeup of a species population is called the **gene pool** and represents not only a source of variance but also genetic relatedness within a group. Any factor that contributes to the frequency of given genes within the population is called *genetic evolution*.

Genetic evolution should not be confused with the evolutionary process that leads to a new species. For this reason, the genetic changes that can take place within a species population are called **microevolution**. In microevolution, a population can develop genetically unique traits but retain membership in the same, larger species of which it is a part. For example, a population of native peoples that has lived in the mountains for many generations might inherit genetic advantages for living at high altitudes. Tourists visiting the Andes Mountains in South America soon find themselves gasping for air. Not so the locals, however, who have adapted to living above 11,000 feet (3,300 m) by having developed higher concentrations of oxygen-carrying hemoglobin in their blood. The Andeans' lungs can grab more oxygen from the air with each breath, effectively counteracting the potential effects of hypoxia—a shortage of oxygen in the blood and the body, also known as altitude sickness. This special genetic trait, restricted to this population, is a form of microevolution.

Several natural forces are at play in microevolution. Natural selection, as originally described by Darwin, is at work at the population level. It operates in conjunction with adaptive change. Biological traits that make an organism better fit to survive are called **adaptations**. If successfully adapted, an organism can stay alive and reproduce. Natural selection and genetics are the mechanisms behind evolution that allow the adaptation of species to environmental forces. Adaptations may protect a species from stressful changes to the habitat, give it speed or agility to avoid **predators**, or provide some biochemical advantage such as resistance to pesticides. An adaptation helps an organism survive so that it can reproduce and pass along its genetic code to another generation.

A **mutation** is any change in the genetic code. Mutations occur at random. They do not occur for a reason, nor do they occur because they are needed. Most mutations are simple errors made by cells when genes are copied, as when new cells are grown or when genetic code is "read" and reproduced by the body to produce proteins. Mutations can also be caused by such environmental factors as damage caused by chemical pollution and genetic irregularities introduced by radioactivity. These causes are less common than random changes due to the body's own normal functions, however.

Mutations can occur in any kind of cell. The only mutations that affect evolution, however, are those that occur in gametes. Mutations are perhaps the most fundamental force underlying genetically based evolutionary factors. Mutations are at work at the population level and can also lead to changes that result in speciation. Every species possesses, by chance, genetic traits that may improve or hinder its chances of survival. The inheritance of biological traits in nature is not under an individual organism's control. In the natural world, an organism cannot dictate which traits it will inherit, nor can its parents direct which traits to pass along. The traits are passed along by chance in the form of mutations—slight, unpredictable variations in the genetic code that happen when organisms reproduce.

Mutations that create an abnormal phenotype may influence the ability of an individual to fit in with others of its species, lessening the chances that that individual will reproduce successfully and pass along its traits to an offspring. On the other hand, a mutation may have a neutral or beneficial effect on the ability of an organism to adapt, making it more likely that such a trait will be passed along to the organism's descendants.

Genetic drift is another factor affecting microevolution. Genetic drift is a chance fluctuation in allele frequency in a gene pool that is not caused by natural selection. Genetic drift is random and figures most importantly in the genetic makeup of small populations. It can occur, for example, if some members of a gene pool die before they are able to reproduce, thus depriving the gene pool of additional variance in the traits that can be inherited and passed on to future generations.

Gene flow, like genetic drift, operates most dramatically in small populations. Gene flow is the introduction of new alleles— additional variety in inheritable traits—from an outside population of the same species.

While genetic drift and gene flow can produce changes in the allele frequency of a population, these changes alone do not necessarily make a population better fit to survive. Natural selection remains the overriding factor that can operate on the genetic variety within a population, no matter if the traits are the result of mutations, genetic drift, or gene flow.

Natural selection is set in motion first by the traits inherited by individuals and then by the interaction of each individual with its habitat. These interconnected processes are sometimes referred to as nature and nurture. Nature provides the traits associated with an organism's genetic makeup. Nurture is the overall effect of the environment on an organism.

MACROEVOLUTION AND SPECIATION

The term *microevolution* refers to changes in the gene pool at a population level. The larger forces of evolution can, however, also lead to the development of entirely new species and a new breeding population. This process of speciation is called **macroevolution.**

As previously noted, a species is defined as a population of organisms that is reproductively isolated from other species.

THINK ABOUT IT

Is There a Reason for Evolution?

Evolution is the result of natural selection and happens by chance. Evolution has no goal or direction but effectively weeds out unfit organisms and selects for those that are better fit—better structured—to survive in their habitat.

Evolution has no particular direction. Evolution does not necessarily progress from simple to more complex forms, as was thought before Darwin. Life simply evolves to adapt to its environment, and there is no intrinsic value placed on one kind of adaptation over another. There are many examples in which organisms adapt to a new environment and then return to a previous environment at a later stage in their evolution. Land animals originally evolved from fish, but there also are cases, such as that of the whale, in which land animals have returned to an aquatic lifestyle. In the southeastern United States, the

Speciation occurs when subgroups within a breeding population become separated. Subgroups that are separated can no longer interbreed. When this occurs, what was once a common gene pool now isolates one population from another, thereby preventing genes from one group from being introduced into the other group. The natural introduction of random mutations causes alleles to appear in one group that do not appear in the other. Over many generations, the forces of natural selection and genetic drift may affect the two populations differently. In time, if the genetic makeup of one group differs significantly from the other, the groups will not be able to interbreed anymore and a new species will have arisen. The time required for speciation to occur is not fixed and will be affected by many factors. These factors range from changes in the

nonvenomous scarlet king snake has adapted coloration that resembles that of the poisonous eastern coral snake. By taking on the appearance of a deadly snake, the harmless scarlet king snake fools predators into leaving it alone. If the scarlet king snake is removed from an environment that it shares with coral snakes, however, natural selection can override such mimicry and promote the evolution of a scarlet king snake that looks less like the coral snake.

Evolution does not always lead to longevity in species. Evolution does not always lead to success or longevity in species when compared with others. There are many examples of organisms, simple and complex, that encountered changes in their environment or other factors to which they could not adequately adapt. The result is extinction.

habitat to the nature of the random genetic mutations that occur in a population.

Theodosius Dobzhansky (1900–1975) was a Ukrainian evolutionary biologist noted for having been at the center of the development of modern evolutionary theory. The result of his work was the so-called *modern evolutionary synthesis*, an approach to explaining evolution through the integration of knowledge from several scientific disciplines, including genetics, biology, and Darwinian evolutionary theory. Dobzhansky was instrumental in defining several reproductive isolating mechanisms—factors that prevent two species from interbreeding, thus helping to maintain the uniqueness of each species. Some of these mechanisms include:

Geographic isolation. Species may not occupy the same habitat. Such **geographic isolation** makes reproductive contact impossible.

Seasonal isolation. Species may have different mating seasons.

Physiological incompatibility. Two different species may have morphologically mismatched sexual organs, making it impossible for two members of different species to interbreed.

Hybrid differences. Two species might be able to mate, but the resulting hybrid fertilized egg does not survive, or the hybrid survives but cannot produce functional gametes. The mule is an infertile hybrid, the cross between a male donkey and a female horse.

Biological Adaptation

Life-forms are sometimes found in the most unlikely places. No matter where one looks on Earth, life seems to have established a foothold. How is it that organisms are able to survive in such varied and often inhospitable environments?

An adaptation is a trait that improves the reproductive success of an organism within a given environment. Adaptation is governed by natural selection. In evolution, the only adaptations that matter are those that can be passed to the next generation.

Some adaptations result from genetic mutations that benefit the survival of an organism. These traits can be passed on to the next generation.

There are two other forms of biological adaptation that are not genetic. They include short-term and long-term biological adaptations that develop during the life of an individual. Prior to the advent of genetic science, the followers of Lamarck incorrectly believed that all kinds of biological adaptations could be passed to the next generation.

Returning to the example of living at high altitudes provides evidence for all three forms of biological adaptation: genetic, short-term, and long-term.

The amount of oxygen in the air thins out at altitudes of more than two miles (3.2 km). People inhale less oxygen with each breath at those elevations. Travelers to such altitudes may experience physiological side effects. A body that is accustomed to having a certain amount of oxygen in the air will tire more quickly when the air is thinner.

The situation becomes even more risky at altitudes of more than 8,125 feet (2,440 m), such as on a mountain or highland plain. At these elevations, a person will get altitude sickness, also known as hypoxia. This is due to low oxygen concentration in the air. Hypoxia can result in headaches, fatigue, dizziness, shortness of breath, loss of appetite, and nausea. At elevations over 25,000 feet (7,575 m), the oxygen is so sparse that hypoxia will kill a person.

Having evolved near sea level, the human body is optimally suited for breathing and functioning at low elevations, where the air is richest with oxygen, from about 50 feet (15 m) above sea level to about 2,000 to 4,000 feet (600 to 1,200 m) above sea level. Most humans do not live at elevations higher than that.

Hypoxia may seem like a biological imperative. Given enough time to adjust, however, humans can adapt their bodies to cope with dangerously thin air. People have three different kinds of biological adaptations to higher altitudes and thinner air.

If a person is new to the mountains, he or she will experience a short-term physiological change. This might include a rapid

THINK ABOUT IT

Of DNA and Genomes

Genome: the complete set of genetic instructions for building an organism.

Genomes are made of DNA and associated protein molecules organized into bundles called chromosomes.

The human genome is estimated to contain 20,000 to 25,000 genes and 3 billion DNA base pairs. These are all stored in 23 pairs of chromosomes.

Every cell in the human body contains 23 pairs of chromosomes.

The human body is made up of about 100 trillion cells.

Different kinds of organisms have different numbers of chromosomes.

Number of Chromosomes in Some Common Plants:

durum wheat, 28

corn (maize), 20

rye, 14

onion, 16

Number of Chromosomes in Some Common Animals:

human, 46

chimpanzee/gorilla, 48

cow, 60

cat, 38

dog, 78

goldfish, 104

fruit fly, 8

heartbeat and shortness of breath as the body adjusts to the thinner air. Breathing more rapidly is a way to inhale an amount of air comparable to that taken in by longer, slower breaths during the same amount of time. When the heart beats faster, it compensates

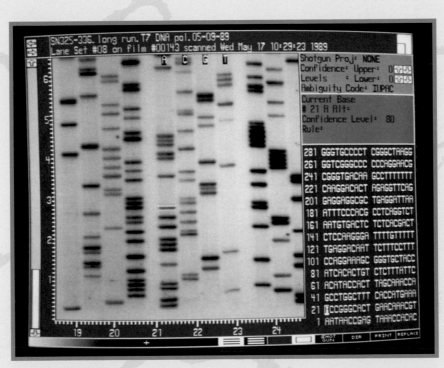

A map of the human genome

The number of genes and chromosomes does not explain every difference between organisms. Humans and apes may share as much as 98 percent of their DNA. The obvious physical and behavioral differences between the two species result from the way that their genetic traits are regulated and expressed.

for less oxygen in the air by pumping the oxygen that *is* available more rapidly, thus fueling tissues and organs at acceptable rates. Rapid breathing and an accelerated heart rate are both ways that the body automatically adjusts to a lower amount of breathable oxygen.

A person born in a lowland area who grows up in a higher-altitude region, or even moves there as an adult, may experience the second kind of biological adaptation, a long-term physiological change that occurs as the person acclimates to the environment. Such a person's lungs and circulatory system can become more efficient at taking oxygen from thin air. A person may develop more red blood cells and vessels to carry oxygen; the person's lungs may grow larger to improve oxygen exchange; and the muscles of the person's respiratory and vascular systems may become stronger to accommodate the processing of oxygen under these more stressful conditions. This change is only for the individual, however, and cannot be passed on genetically.

The third kind of biological adaptation is a genetic one that is transferred from one generation to the next through DNA. A group of native peoples that has lived in the mountains for many generations might inherit genetic advantages for living at high altitudes.

The accompanying table summarizes the three forms of biological adaptation using this example.

In addition to the three forms of biological adaptation, humans have the unique ability to make additional adaptations using technology. Clothing is a simple but effective technology for adapting to different climates. Other technological adaptations are dazzling, such as the creation of space craft, submarines, and other portable environments to protect human life in places where it cannot survive without help.

The Rate of Evolution

Darwin viewed evolution and the emergence of new species as a slow and gradual process. In his view, it took thousands and even

FORMS OF BIOLOGICAL ADAPTATION

The following table shows three ways that humans adapt biologically to their environment.

Type of Adaptation	Cause	Example
Short-term physiological change	Occurs naturally when an organism encounters a change to its environment	Body adapts by faster heart rate, taking gulps of air (hyperventilation)
Long-term physiological change	Occurs during the growth stage of an individual organism or during long-term exposure to a new or changing environment	Respiratory system becomes better at extracting oxygen from thin air
Genetic change	Occurs over many generations	Larger chest cavity of native highlanders is able to absorb more oxygen from thin air

millions of years to create a new species. This view is called gradualism. Gradualism assumes that slow and gradual changes over a long period of time lead to major biological changes to a species. The fossil record does indeed provide many clues to such gradual changes.

The concept of gradualism was challenged in 1972 by a bold new idea proposed by paleontologists Stephen Jay Gould (1941–2002) and Niles Eldredge (b. 1943). Gould and Eldredge still assumed that natural selection was the underlying machinery of evolution, but they noticed that evolution does not always occur at a slow and gradual pace, even by geologic standards. The fossil record shows that many species can go for millions of years without any significant change. It is as if evolution were standing still for some species. Living examples, such as the cockroach and bowfin fish, seem to follow this pattern, having not changed significantly for many millions of years. This can change, however, if a population of a given species suddenly encounters a dramatic change to its habitat. Such a change might be caused by a geological event, a change in climate, or even interaction with other species. Following such an occurrence, a short period of rapid evolution may take place that affects a subgroup of a species population. Those individuals with certain traits favoring their survival may change dramatically over a period of tens of thousands or several million years—mere seconds and minutes on the scale of geologic time. The changes may result in new species. This rapid twist to the evolutionary story is called **punctuated equilibria.**

The evidence for punctuated equilibria is usually found in a small portion of an overall species population. For example, when insects are exposed to pesticides, certain members of the population can rapidly develop resistance. The same can be said of bacteria that grow resistant to antibiotic medicines. These adaptations are the result of natural selection. Such changes can mark the beginning of the development of a new species.

The fossil record of the flowering plants provides a dramatic example of evolutionary opportunism and the influence of one species of life on another. Prior to the appearance of flowering plants about 140 million years ago, the world landscape was dominated by seed-bearing plants such as conifers, ginkgos, ferns, and palms. These plants reproduce by simply dropping their seeds. Flowering plants cannot reproduce without pollination, the physical transmittal of a plant's pollen so that it comes into contact with a plant's seed. Although this reproductive complication might seem too daunting for a new plant species to overcome, flowering plants actually rose and diversified rapidly. This rapid rise and diversification are revealed by an abundant fossil record of leaves and pollen.

The first leaves of flowering plants were shaped simply and had poorly organized veins. The earliest examples of pollen also were primitive, with an unadorned surface structure. As time went on, both leaves and pollen evolved more complex structures that aided their survival. Leaf structures became broader and varied in shape, with geometrically laid-out veins—features that added to the robustness of the plants. Pollen began to exhibit a more sculpted surface texture that was more easily grabbed by the other organisms that were transporting the pollen to facilitate pollination. The rise of flowering plants to the position of the most dominant form of vegetation took only about 10 million years. This rapid spread was most likely due to the role played by birds and insects in the process of pollination.

What can be concluded from this evidence is that the rate of evolution for any given species will vary depending on the biologic, geographic, and environmental circumstances affecting a population of organisms. The rate may be slow and gradual, as Darwin thought, or rapid as Gould and Eldredge suggested. The facts favor a wide range of evolutionary rates on a spectrum represented by gradualism at one end and punctuated equilibria at the other.

CONCLUSION

Darwin's mechanism of natural selection has proved to be a durable explanation for the way species change over time. Ample support for evolution comes from several disciplines—disciplines as distinct as molecular biology, paleontology, mathematics, and quantum physics. The evidence converges on a stark realization about the nature of life. All species participate in a process called evolution that never abates. What is happening today in the cells and genetic architecture of every living organism may influence, in a small part, the continued development of that organism's species. The study of evolution provides some answers to humans' most profound questions about where life comes from. The study of evolution also has greatly influenced the ways that humans view, understand, and classify other organisms in the world. It is only through evolution that the many branches of Earth's family tree can be linked, starting from the first single-celled organisms that sprouted 3.5 billion years ago.

Section Two of *Primates and Human Ancestors* explores the evolutionary roots of the human family tree and the story of the primates.

SUMMARY

This chapter described the biological principles underlying evolution.

1. Gregor Mendel's groundbreaking work in the breeding of pea plants laid the foundation for the science of genetics even though he, like Darwin, had no knowledge about the biochemical basis of inheritance. The resulting patterns that he discovered are known as Mendelian genetics.

2. Among Mendel's discoveries were that discrete "particulate factors" (genes) were responsible for inheritance, that offspring possess two genes for each trait (one from each parent), and that genes may come in versions that are different, called alleles.

3. Having two of the same alleles for a given gene (trait) is known as being homozygous. Having a pair of nonmatching alleles for a gene is a condition known as heterozygous.

4. The genotype determines which trait will be expressed. The observable trait is known as the phenotype.

5. A recessive allele, or trait, is not destroyed and may be expressed in a later generation.

6. Genetic material contains all of the instructions needed to construct an entire organism. Genetic material can be passed from parent to offspring and then from cell to cell during the process of cell division. Genetic material can make exact copies of itself. Genetic material represents the entire range of possible variation within a species.

7. DNA (short for *deoxyribonucleic acid*) is the molecule that carries genetic code. Genes are located in chromosomes on strands of DNA.

8. Population genetics is the study of the frequency of alleles, genotypes, and phenotypes in a given group of individuals. The combined genetic makeup of a population is called the gene pool.

9. The genetic changes that can take place within a population is called microevolution.

10. Natural selection and genetics are the mechanisms behind evolution that allow the adaptation of species to environmental forces.

11. A mutation is any change in the genetic code. Mutations occur at random.

12. The process of speciation is also called macroevolution.

13. A genome is the complete set of genetic change instructions for building an organism.

14. Three forms of biological adaptation are genetic change and short-term and long-term physiological changes; the latter two forms are not transmittable to offspring.

15. Gradualism assumes that slow and gradual changes over a long period of time lead to major biological changes to a species. Punctuated equilibria is an occasional acceleration in the evolution of a species because of specific environmental stresses.

SECTION TWO:
PRIMATES

ORIGIN AND CLASSIFICATION OF THE PRIMATES

Primates are members of the order Archonta, a somewhat loosely knit contingent of **eutherian** mammal groups that appear to be related, although the evolutionary links between them are not fully understood.

The earliest members of the Archonta arose in North America and Europe during the Paleocene and Eocene Epochs. At the base of the primate family tree were the Plesiadapiformes, an extinct group that consisted of the most primitive **taxa** associated with early archontans. Plesiadapiforms were long-snouted quadrupeds with long tails and squirrel-like limbs equipped with claws for climbing trees. Their jaws and teeth were rodentlike, and they had long incisors (front teeth). The Plesiadapiform dental formula was similar to that of the earliest primates, but the **postcranial** skeleton of the plesiadapiforms was more like that of flying lemurs.

Primates traditionally have been divided into two major groups for classifying purposes. The **prosimians** ("before monkeys") include lower primates with a more squirrel-like body. This group includes the lemurs and the lorises. The animals in this group are the most primitive primates.

The **anthropoids** ("man structure") or so-called higher primates include the tarsiers; New World monkeys (from the Americas); Old World monkeys (from Africa, Asia, and Europe); apes; and humans. Of these, the small tarsier is the most primitive of the anthropoids and may represent a **transitional** form between the lower primates (prosimians) and higher primates.

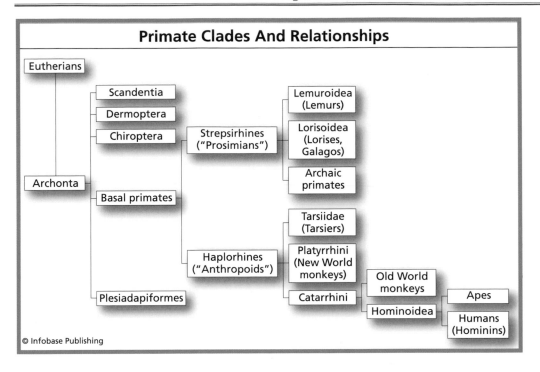

Primate Clades And Relationships

Eutherians

Archonta
- Scandentia
- Dermoptera
- Chiroptera
- Basal primates
- Plesiadapiformes

Strepsirhines ("Prosimians")
- Lemuroidea (Lemurs)
- Lorisoidea (Lorises, Galagos)
- Archaic primates

Haplorhines ("Anthropoids")
- Tarsiidae (Tarsiers)
- Platyrrhini (New World monkeys)
- Catarrhini
  - Old World monkeys
  - Hominoidea
    - Apes
    - Humans (Hominins)

© Infobase Publishing

Recent fossil discoveries, morphological analysis, and molecular data have led to a rethinking of primate classification. This reassessment has resulted in a revised classification that is widely accepted today. This new view has removed the tarsiers from the prosimians and placed them in the group formerly known as the anthropoids. In this revised classification, the term *strepsirhine* is substituted for *prosimian* and the term *haplorhine* is substituted for *anthropoid*. This revision is based on a more refined definition of each group that combines current knowledge of fossils and molecular analysis. This rethought classification is illustrated in the diagram "Primate Clades and Relationships."

The fossil record of primates indicates that strepsirhines first evolved about 60 million years ago and provided the stock from which the haplorhines arose, 45 million to 50 million years ago. The precise evolutionary links between strepsirhines and haplorhines as well as the geographic origin of primates are not well understood yet from the fossil record and have become hotly contested issues among paleontologists. The earliest primate fossils are found in North Africa (Morocco). The scanty Eocene fossil record on that continent has gaps, however, thus making it impossible to test whether primates first diversified in Africa (the "Out of Africa" scenario). As with most groups of placental mammals, paleontologists suspect that primates originated and first evolved in southern Asia during the Late Cretaceous or Paleocene Epoch before dispersing into other continents. They then probably moved on to other continents—including Europe, Africa, and North America—during the Eocene Epoch.

Strepsirhines

The strepsirhines include the living lemurs of Madagascar and the lorises and galagos from tropical Asia and Africa. These small to medium-sized lower primates retain some of the primitive features seen in the plesiadapiforms and the oldest primates. Most strepsirhines have a highly developed sense of smell and keen eyesight. The protruding incisors of strepsirhines form a dental specialization called a tooth comb that is used primarily for grooming. While most of their digits have fingernails, some taxa have special claws on their toes that are used for grooming. Strepsirhines live in trees. The animals have grasping hands and feet but have poorly opposed thumbs. This limits the daredevil nature of their swinging from limb to limb. Strepsirhines move about primarily as quadrupedal animals. Unlike the highly social haplorhines, strepsirhines are more solitary creatures and lack the social behavior patterns seen in higher primates.

Strepsirhines have a poor fossil record prior to the Late Pleistocene. Lemurs once roamed widely across Africa, North America, and Europe but are found today only on the islands of Madagascar and Comoros. The lorises have a fossil record that dates back the Eocene of Africa. Today, lorises are found in tropical regions of Africa and Asia.

Because **extant** lemurs are agile, cat-sized creatures that live in trees, it is surprising to find that there once existed a line of lemurs that were as big as orangutans and gorillas and that lumbered slowly through the trees and along the ground. The geographic isolation of

Madagascar from mainland Africa gave lemurs a chance to diversify rapidly and occupy ecological niches filled on the continent of Africa by monkeys, apes, and other **herbivores**. There also were fewer predators on Madagascar; this gave lemurs the chance to fully exploit their habitat.

Haplorhines

The haplorhines, or anthropoids, were well established in Africa, Europe, and Asia by about 25 million years ago. Their actual origins must have been earlier, and it generally has been agreed that the higher primates were descendants of Eocene strepsirhines. The haplorhines are the most highly social of primates. All but one species, the orangutan, live in social groups, and even solitary orangutans persist in maintaining regular contact with others of their kind. Most haplorhines are also **diurnal**—active during the day.

Haplorhines include all living anthropoids, nonhuman and human, as well as their extinct forms.

Living anthropoids are classified into two large groups: the catarrhines ("downward facing noses")—which include Old World monkeys, apes, and hominins—and the platyrrhines ("flat noses"), or New World monkeys. These groups represent an evolutionary divergence that occurred when ancestral primates began to divide into increasingly specialized subgroups.

The catarrhines share several traits, including closely spaced nostrils that point downward and only eight permanent premolars: two upper and two lower on either side of the jaw. Catarrhines are divided further into two additional subgroups, the Old World monkeys and the Hominoidea, which consist of apes and hominins (human ancestors and humans). On average, catarrhines are much larger than platyrrhines and have a dental formula that includes long, pointed canine teeth and a gap between the lower front teeth that allows the canines to self sharpen by rubbing against the lower premolars.

The platyrrhines consist only of what are called New World monkeys. This distinction separates haplorhine primates from the "old" world of Africa (and, some might say, Asia), where anthropoids originated, from haplorhine primates found in the "new" world of the Americas. New World monkeys are distinguished by having widely spaced, round nostrils that point outward and by having a total of 12 permanent premolars: three upper and three lower on either side of the jaw.

Molecular evidence suggests that ancestral anthropoids slowly began to diverge into the catarrhines and the platyrrhines about 40 million years ago. The first fossil evidence of this split includes the appearance of extinct New World monkeys in South America between 30 million and 35 million years ago. While the New World monkeys have retained a relatively stable body plan and lifestyle since the Oligocene, the catarrhine branch of anthropoids has diverged further into several different groups. These include the Old World monkeys, the gibbons, the orangutans, the gorillas, the chimpanzees, and humans.

By the beginning of the Miocene, primate populations were largely isolated on their respective continents. The Old World monkeys and early anthropoids were in Africa, India, Southeast Asia, and Japan; the New World monkeys were in South and Central America. This concentration of primate populations led to an explosion of evolutionary trends in Africa. The main product of this evolutionary explosion was the rapid rise of the apes and the eventual appearance of humans.

EMERGENCE OF ANTHROPOIDS AND ANCESTRAL HUMANS

Early primates were successful largely because they were able to adapt quickly to environmental changes that were transforming the world. Survival of the primates hinged on several important anatomical changes. These changes included stereoscopic vision, specialized dental formulas, and the modifications to limb structure that empowered the animals' mobility, not only in the trees but also on the ground. The modification of the primate jaw was an especially important key to primate adaptability. As their upper

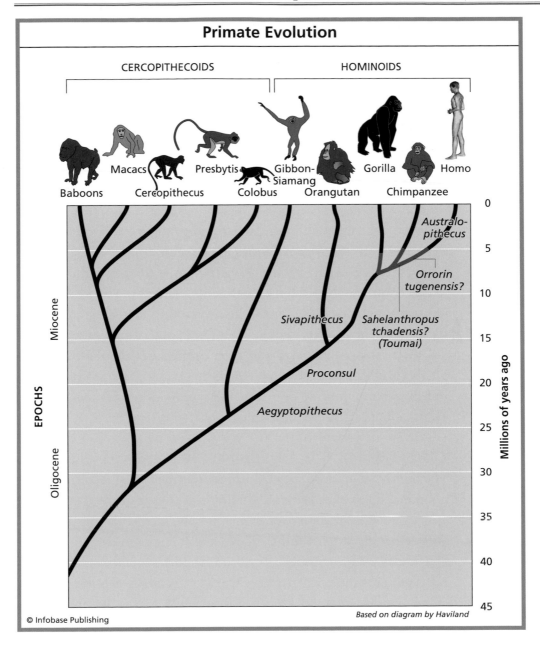

Primate Evolution

CERCOPITHECOIDS   HOMINOIDS

Baboons   Macacs   Cercopithecus   Presbytis   Colobus   Gibbon-Siamang   Orangutan   Gorilla   Chimpanzee   Homo

Australo-pithecus

Orrorin tugenensis?

Sivapithecus   Sahelanthropus tchadensis? (Toumai)

Proconsul

Aegyptopithecus

Miocene

Oligocene

EPOCHS

Millions of years ago

0   5   10   15   20   25   30   35   40   45

© Infobase Publishing   *Based on diagram by Haviland*

and lower jaws and related musculature became stronger, primates were able to chew tougher foods. This widened their dietary choices. Paleoanthropologist Craig Stanford hypothesizes the improvement of primate jaws a step further when he suggests that stronger jaws led to the ingestion of more food and to the gradual development of larger body size.

With the passing of the Oligocene Epoch, the face of the Earth and its habitats were transformed dramatically from what had been the warm, tropical Eocene world that had spawned the early radiation of primates. The continents drifted farther apart. North America became isolated from Europe. India, once a drifting island, fused with Asia. Africa became geographically isolated from most of Eurasia. A cooling trend that largely affected the Northern Hemisphere made the once-tropical habitats of North America, Europe, and Asia inhospitable for primates, and primates subsequently disappeared from many areas above the equator.

By the beginning of the Miocene, primate populations were largely isolated on different continents. The Old World monkeys and early anthropoids were in Africa, India, Southeast Asia, and Japan. The New World monkeys were in South and Central America. This regionalized concentration of primate populations led to an explosion of evolutionary trends in Africa. The main product of this evolutionary activity was the rapid rise of the apes and the eventual appearance of humans.

The Prosimian–Anthropoid Divergence

The higher primates—the haplorhines (anthropoids)—consist of the monkeys, apes, and humans. Anatomical trends of the haplorhines as compared with the lower primates—the strepshirhines (prosimians)—include larger brains, an eye socket enclosed by a bony orbit, a fusion of the bones of the skull cap, a shortened face, and a different dental formula. Prosimians are also primarily arboreal, or tree living, having adapted long limbs, clawlike nails, and prehensile tails in many species. No anthropoids developed prehensile tails, and there is a tendency in this group toward large body size and a ground-based lifestyle with some tree climbing.

The early anthropoids appeared in the middle Eocene and were more monkeylike than the great apes we picture today. Many of the features associated with apes today were not yet well developed in

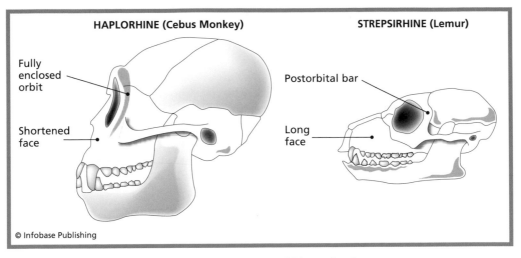

Differences in the skulls of haplorhine and strepsirhine primates

the **basal** apes. The earliest known fossils of apes often consist only of teeth and jaws. The oldest known fossils believed to be those of an early anthropoid consist of several molar teeth of *Algeripithecus* (Middle Eocene, Algeria). While the occurrence of these fossils in North Africa has argued for an "Out of Africa" origin for the haplorhines, the discovery of an equally old and more informative primate specimen from China has complicated this view. The remains of *Eosimias* ("dawn monkey") were discovered by a joint American-Chinese paleontological team between 1994 and 1997. The remains consist of jaw and skull fragments as well as pieces of limb and ankle bones.

Eosimias was a tiny primate, as small as a pygmy marmoset—about 6 inches (15 cm) excluding the tail. Its remains show that many anthropoid traits of the skull and teeth were evolving prior to the attainment of the larger body size associated with most higher primates. The teeth of *Eosimias* were more primitive than those of *Algeripithecus* from North Africa, which suggests that *Eosimias* represented a more ancient branch of anthropoid lineage.

The discovery of *Eosimias* in Asia has great implications for the "Out of Africa" theory of haplorhine origins. Christopher Beard of the Carnegie Museum of Natural History was the expedition leader of the team that discovered *Eosimias*. According to Beard, "The fact that *Eosimias* was so much more primitive than roughly contemporary African higher primates was potentially one of its most important attributes from a scientific perspective." Beard explains further: "First, the presence of the most primitive higher primates in China could mean that higher primates actually originated on the Asian landmass, thus bursting the bubble of the 'Out of Africa' hypothesis."

The existence of early anthropoids is much clearer a little later in the fossil record. One significant source of early haplorhine fossils is the Fayum Depression, a geologic formation in Egypt. The fossils from this locality date from the Late Eocene and Early Oligocene. The Fayum Depression is located in the Sahara Desert. The area once was a lush, tropical forest divided by rivers, however, and was home to many kinds of plants and animals. The Fayum Depression is noted for its fossil remains, although most are fragmentary. Among these are several undisputed taxa of extinct anthropoids that include *Oligopithecus*, *Proteopithecus*, and *Catopithecus*. Like *Eosimias*, these primates contained a mosaic of primitive and more **derived** features of haplorhines.

The fossil record of prosimians and anthropoids show that even as far back as 45 million years ago, the two lineages of primates were well established and often were living in the same regions. The ancestral origins of the two lineages were probably the same. The divergence of anthropoid species from prosimian species was a gradual one. The development of larger brains and a modified dental formula—so significant to distinguishing anthropoids from prosimians—came later in the evolution of the early apes. This suggests that other traits may have played a more important role in this divergence. Modifications of the limbs and supporting skeletal structures gradually converted the apes from a predominantly tree-borne lifestyle to one that was more ground based. Anatomical evidence also shows more **sexual dimorphism** in early apes. Such visible differences between the size and physiological features of males and females suggests the emergence of more sophisticated social behavior in early apes, a feature that may have improved their survival potential. The topic of primate social behavior is discussed in more detail in Chapter 4.

The diversification of early apes progressed rapidly between the Early Miocene Epoch and the beginning of the Pliocene Epoch, a span ranging from about 23 million to 5 million years ago.

Apes (Hominoidea)

The Hominoidea, or apes, today include the gorillas and chimpanzees from Africa, the gibbons and orangutans from Asia, and humans. The hub of ape evolution was eastern Africa, along the area where the Great Rift Valley was developing. The earliest fossils of true apes are known from Kenya, Namibia, Uganda, and Ethiopia. Apes of the Miocene formed a much more diverse group than apes do today. Miocene apes were forest dwellers and primarily fruit eaters, and they lived in an environment that was largely forested. Whereas living apes are restricted to just four taxa, Miocene apes are known from dozens of taxa. The earliest apes typically had bodies similar to those of monkeys but skulls and a dental formula that were apelike. Most of the earliest apes were quadrupeds. Because of their small eyes, they were most likely diurnal.

The ancestors of modern apes arose during the Middle Miocene. Some kinds of apes migrated to the north to populate Europe and Asia. By the Late Miocene, human ancestors had diverged from the lineages of gorillas and chimpanzees.

The quest to determine which Miocene apes were the direct ancestors of humans is at the center of an ongoing debate in the study of primate evolution. The following are representative taxa of extinct apes, some of which come close to fulfilling the goal of that quest. A discussion of the earliest humans begins in Chapter 5.

Extinct Apes

Proconsul (Early Miocene, Africa). The most abundant group of hominoids from the Early Miocene belongs to the taxon *Proconsul*

(continues on page 76)

THINK ABOUT IT

DNA Evidence for the Origins of Primate Groups

Evidence for the evolutionary relationships between organisms comes from many sources. Traditionally, the **phylogeny**—the family tree based on shared, inherited traits—for any lineage of organism has been based on an accumulation of evidence from the fossil record. In the case of fossils, to know the geologic time and location for a given fossil animal is of key importance. With that knowledge, a case can be made for the ancestral relationships of a given lineage. This is done by comparing the sequence of fossils for the presence of traits that may have been inherited from earlier members of the clan.

In many cases, the fossil record simply lacks the kind of evidence needed to put the pieces of the evolutionary story together. The use of molecular phylogenetic methods offers an option for filling in some of these gaps.

A phylogenetic analysis based on molecular evidence uses information derived from genes or proteins of living species to determine when in the past such species may have diverged from ancestral groups. This work is done statistically, using data derived from such techniques as DNA sequencing to compare the composition of molecules from different species. In 1969, anthropologist Vincent Sarich and biochemist Allan Wilson compared amino acid sequences of hemoglobins—the oxygen-carrying component of red blood cells—from humans, chimpanzees, gorillas, and rhesus monkeys as the basis for determining when, in the past, these lineages most likely diverged into separate species.

By knowing that genetic differences between species require time to accumulate, the two scientists originated the concept of the **molecular clock** to detect when related species branched away from each other in the far past. For this mathematical clock to work, the scientists needed to calibrate it to a known point in the fossil record when a specific divergence between species took place. By comparing a verifiable fossil date with the composition of the present-day genetic molecules of a species, Wilson and Sarich ascertained a rate at which molecular change took

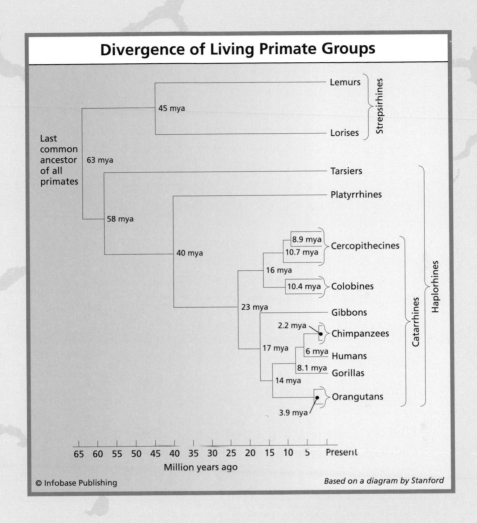

Divergence of Living Primate Groups

Last common ancestor of all primates

63 mya

45 mya — Lemurs / Lorises (Strepsirhines)

58 mya

Tarsiers

40 mya — Platyrrhines

23 mya

16 mya

8.9 mya / 10.7 mya — Cercopithecines

10.4 mya — Colobines

Gibbons

17 mya

2.2 mya — Chimpanzees

6 mya — Humans

8.1 mya — Gorillas

14 mya

3.9 mya — Orangutans

Catarrhines | Haplorhines

Million years ago: 65 60 55 50 45 40 35 30 25 20 15 10 5 Present

© Infobase Publishing

Based on a diagram by Stanford

place. This was a revolutionary approach to phylogeny at the time, but Wilson and Sarich were quite confident that their methods would stand the test of time. They suggested that their molecular clock placed the divergence of ancestral humans from apes at about 5 million years ago.

(continues)

(continued)

They also came to the bold conclusion that, "Indeed, our calculations indicate that it is difficult to consider seriously any date in excess of 10 million years for the origin of the hominid lineage."

The Wilson-Sarich model has held up pretty well over the years. Much research in molecular phylogeny has been done during the intervening years. Humans are most closely related to the genus *Pan*, or chimpanzee. Techniques for using DNA and genomes as a source to extrapolate the timing of the *Pan*-human evolutionary split have grown increasingly sophisticated since the work of Wilson and Sarich. Today, the consensus is that ancestral humans split from the great apes somewhere between 5 million and 7 million years ago, at the end of the Miocene Epoch.

As paleoanthropologist Craig Stanford points out, the goal of molecular phylogeny is not to replace the traditional phylogenies developed by comparing actual fossil specimens. Ideally, both methods eventually will converge on the same conclusions.

(continued from page 73)

("before Consul"). The original specimen was named in 1933 for Consul, a popular performing chimpanzee in Europe. A 1947 expedition to the Lake Victoria area of Kenya, mounted by anthropologists Louis Leakey (1903–1972) and his wife Mary Leakey (1913–1996), resulted in the spectacular find, by Mary Leakey, of a fairly complete specimen of *Proconsul*. The discovery and study of *Proconsul* represented an important contribution to the study of hominoid and even human evolution. Louis Leakey said of *Proconsul* that it seemed to be "neither an ancestral ape, nor yet an ancestor of man, but a side branch with characteristics of both stocks." This rational assessment has stood the test of time, even as many more Miocene hominoids have been discovered.

Proconsul is known from three species that range in weight from about 24 pounds to about 190 pounds (10.9 to 86.7 kg). With a long back and slender limbs, the *Proconsul* body was much more like that of a monkey than that of a modern ape. *Proconsul* lacked a tail, however. Its skull and teeth were more apelike, with hominoid dentition. It probably lived in trees and was adept at swinging from branch to branch.

Proconsul once was considered the last common ancestor held by apes and Old World monkeys, but that distinction now may go to another Miocene hominoid, *Morotopithecus* (Early Miocene, Uganda). *Morotopithecus* includes an even more radical mosaic of monkeylike and apelike features than *Proconsul*. Specifically, the dentition of *Morotopithecus* is less derived and more like that of monkeys than that of apes, and the postcranial skeleton of *Morotopithecus* features a shorter, stiffer back and a shoulder girdle better adapted for apelike arm swinging than for **brachiation**.

Afropithecus (Middle Miocene, Africa). Weighing an average of 110 pounds (50 kg), *Afropithecus* was a moderately large hominoid. It is known from fragments of its skull, jaw, and skeleton. *Afropithecus* had a long, narrow snout; relatively small eyes; and robust, tusklike canine teeth. The protruding upper incisors were wide and flat and appear to have worked in concert with the large canines to gather and grind hard seeds and nuts. *Afropithecus* is considered close to the origins of modern hominoids.

Sivapithecus (Late Miocene, Africa, Europe, and Asia). *Sivapithecus* represents a line of Miocene hominoids that radiated widely after the land bridge between Africa and Eurasia was reestablished during the Middle Miocene. *Sivapithecus* was discovered first in India and Pakistan, but examples have been found since in such widely separated regions as Turkey, Kenya, and China. The facial and dental traits of *Sivapithecus* were similar to those of the living orangutan, and it is likely that *Sivapithecus* was ancestral to the modern lineage of Asian great apes. The body of *Sivapithecus* was not very orangutanlike, however, and it had grasping feet more like those of the chimpanzee. *Sivapithecus* measured about 5 feet

(1.5 m) tall. The thick enamel of its teeth indicates that *Sivapithecus* fed largely on hard foods such as nuts and seeds.

Dryopithecus (Middle to Late Miocene, Africa, Europe, and Asia). One line of European hominoids is represented by *Dryopithecus*, part of a group that may have included the common ancestor of the modern gibbons and great apes (chimpanzees and gorillas). *Dryopithecus*, which had typically hominoid molars, was a small, tree-climbing animal adapted to eating fruit. *Dryopithecus* measured about 24 inches (60 cm) long. It had a body more like that of a chimpanzee than that of a monkey, so although *Dryopithecus* was most certainly a good climber, it also was well adapted for moving about on the ground. This adaptation would have been important in the Late Miocene world as grasslands and open expanses of land became more common.

Pierolapithecus (Middle Miocene, Spain). *Pierolapithecus* is currently one of the best candidates for a group that consists of the last common ancestors of the great apes and humans. *Pierolapithecus* existed at just about the time that apes diverged from other hominoids. An excellent specimen of *Pierolapithecus* that consists of skull parts, hands, feet, vertebrae, and other fragments appears to represent a single adult male that may have weighed about 75 pounds (34 kg). Its flat rib cage, stiff lower spine, and flexible wrists and shoulder girdle made it adaptable for tree climbing as well as for so-called knuckle walking while on the ground.

Gigantopithecus (Late Miocene to Pleistocene, China, India, and Pakistan). The largest of all known apes was *Gigantopithecus*, a monstrous primate that probably was most like an orangutan. It is known only from fragmentary fossils that include jaws and teeth. When these fragmentary remains are scaled up to predict body proportions, some estimates make *Gigantopithecus* as much as 10 feet (3 m) tall, with a weight of 1,200 pounds (545 kg). As big as it was, *Gigantopithecus* probably subsisted on such tough vegetation as bamboo, nuts, and seeds, as well as on fruit. The last of the line of these giant apes died out only about 300,000 years ago, a time that they shared with early humans.

An illustration of *Dryopithecus*

CONCLUSION

The fossil record of primates provides a robust picture of their evolution, including the division of the prosimians and anthropoids and the development of Old World monkeys, apes, and ancestral humans. Molecular phylogenetic methods affirm evidence from the fossil record by showing that ancestral humans most likely diverged from the apes between 5 million and 7 million years ago. Chapter 4 examines the anatomical and behavioral traits that make primates unique among mammals. This examination leads to the introduction of the human primate in Section Three.

SUMMARY

This chapter examined the evolution of the primates and especially the lineage of primates known as anthropoids.

1. Primates are members of an order of eutherian mammals known as the Archonta. The earliest members of the Archonta arose in North America and Europe during the Paleocene and Eocene Epochs.

2. At the base of the primate family tree were the Plesiadapiformes, an extinct group that consisted of the most primitive taxa associated with early archontans.

3. Primates traditionally have been divided into two major groups for classifying purposes. The prosimians ("before monkeys") include lower primates with a more squirrel-like body, including the lemurs and the lorises. These strepsirhines are the most primitive primates. The anthropoids ("man structure"), or so-called higher primates, include the tarsiers; New World monkeys (from the Americas); Old World monkeys (from Africa, Asia, and Europe); apes; and humans. Modern taxonomic nomenclature substitutes the term *strepsirhine* for *prosimian* and the term *haplorhine* for *anthropoid*.

4. Living anthropoids are classified into two large groups: the catarrhines ("downward facing noses"), which include Old World monkeys, apes, and hominins, and the platyrrhines ("flat noses"), or New World monkeys.

5. The hub of ape evolution was eastern Africa, along the area where the Great Rift Valley was developing. The earliest fossils of true apes are known from Kenya, Namibia, Uganda, and Ethiopia.

6. Early primates were successful largely because they were able to adapt quickly to environmental changes that were transforming the world. By the beginning of the Miocene, primate populations were largely isolated on different continents.

7. The higher primates—the haplorhines, or anthropoids—consist of the monkeys, the apes, and humans. Anatomical trends of the haplorhines as compared with the lower primates—the strepshirhines, or prosimians—include larger brains, an eye socket enclosed by a bony orbit, a fusion of the

bones of the skull cap, a shortened face, and a different dental formula.

8. The early anthropoids appeared in the middle Eocene and were more monkeylike than the great apes we see today.

9. The discovery of the tiny primate *Eosimias* in Asia offers evidence contrary to the traditional "Out of Africa" theory of haplorhine origins.

10. The emergence of ancestral humans from apes took place between 5 million and 7 million years ago.

4

Primate Biology and Behavior

Soon after the publication of his book *On the Origin of Species* in 1859, Charles Darwin was faced with having to address the application of his theory to the evolution of humankind. Although he had for many years given consideration to human origins, Darwin had decided not to publish these ideas in *On the Origin of Species*. He was admittedly reluctant to do so because it would "only add to the prejudices" against his own views. Although Darwin had gingerly avoided such a discussion in his most famous book, critics and supporters alike immediately entered the fray to make the case for or against the evolution, through natural selection, of the human species from primates.

Among the controversies was one of classification. If humans were, in fact, members of the mammal group known as primates, on what basis were they different from other members of the group? Although the answer might seem obvious on the surface, the scientific basis for defining humans as a member of the primates was a topic of fundamental importance to the community of nineteenth century naturalists. It was this discussion that led to the science of human origins and cemented the validity of evolution as the keystone of biological science.

The eminent British naturalist Thomas Huxley (1825–1895), an avid champion of Darwin's work, was one of the most energetic early contributors to thought about human origins. Darwin, when he finally decided to publish a book about human evolution in 1871, acknowledged the contributions of Huxley by saying:

It would be beyond my limits, and quite beyond my knowledge, even to name the innumerable points of structure in which man agrees with the other primates. Our great anatomist and philosopher, Prof. Huxley, has fully discussed this subject, and concludes that man in all parts of his organization differs less from the higher apes, than these do from the lower members of the same group. Consequently there 'is no justification for placing man in a distinct order.'

Huxley established an early classification of primates that divided them into three groups, all with a common ancestor: the lemurs, monkeys of all kinds, and apes (including humans) alone. While today's understanding of primate classification now contains several other subgroups and divisions, Huxley basically had the right idea. Ever since, humans have widely been accepted as primates, the order of mammals that has arguably had a greater impact on life on Earth—for better or for worse—than any other mammal order.

This chapter explores the biological and behavioral nature of primates. For a complete discussion of nonhuman primate origins, readers may wish to read another book in this series, *The Age of Mammals*. A detailed view of human **anatomy** is discussed in the book *Early Humans*, also part of *The Prehistoric Earth*.

BIOLOGICAL CHARACTERISTICS OF PRIMATES

Humans are one of more than 200 kinds of living primates in the world today. Primates ("of the first") include the biological group made up of all lemurs, monkeys, and apes, including humans. Primates live today in tropical regions of the Americas, Africa, and Asia. Humans, of course, have used technology to adapt to living conditions anywhere on the planet.

Primates range widely in size, from the largest gorillas, which weigh 500 pounds (225 kg), to the chipmunk-sized dwarf bush baby, which weighs a mere 2.3 ounces (65 grams). Many primates are social creatures, but there are some that prefer to live alone.

Primates also vary in their degree of intelligence; in whether they are most active during the day or at night; and in their dietary preferences, which range from fruits, leaves, and nuts to a more **omnivorous** diet to which a good proportion of insects and meat have been added.

Primates are distinguished from other mammals by several anatomical traits related to their limbs, posture, and locomotion; diet and teeth; and brain and senses.

Limbs, Posture, and Locomotion

One of the most familiar and defining anatomical structures of primates is the grasping hand and, in some species, grasping feet. This is due to the presence in all primates of an **opposable** thumb on the hand, and, in some, an opposable big toe on the foot. Each hand or foot has five digits. The presence of a thumb or big toe that can flex against—that is, in opposition to—the other digits makes it possible for a primate to grasp objects.

The degree to which the thumb or big toe is useful for grasping varies, depending on the kind of primate. In spider monkeys and gibbons, for example, the thumb is greatly reduced and the fingers elongated to such a degree that grasping is not possible. In humans, the big toe barely functions for grasping, whereas in nonhuman primates, such as apes, the big toe makes the foot as useful for grasping as the hand.

Having grasping hands and feet enables primates to take advantage of several strategies for moving about. Vertical clingers or leapers use their hands and feet to jump from branch to branch in trees. Some rely primarily on arm swinging, or brachiation, in which the body is fully supported by either **forelimb** as the animal swings from branch to branch. Other primates, including the apes, use their arm strength to pull themselves up by the arms to hang and climb. Most primates other than humans are quadrupedal when on the ground, walking on all fours. Asian orangutans walk on their fists; African apes walk on their knuckles.

Foot Skeletons

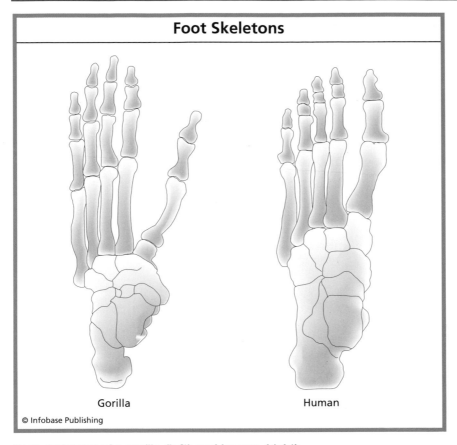

Gorilla   Human

© Infobase Publishing

Foot skeletons of a gorilla (*left*) and human (*right*)

In humans, the foot is flatter than in other primates, and the toes are arranged on the same plane, reducing the ability to grasp in favor of the ability to walk upright.

Primate digits also have flat nails instead of claws. This distinguishes them from the digits of other climbing animals such as tree shrews and squirrels. The primate's sense of touch is also enhanced by the presence of fibrous pads at the ends of the digits.

Although most primates other than humans do not normally stand erect, their skeletal design has a tendency toward an upright posture. This is especially true because of the long spine of the upper body. Upright posture can be expressed in many ways aside from standing. It may be expressed while sitting, leaping, and walking.

Diet and Teeth

There is a strong tendency toward omnivory in primates, and their tooth pattern, though **heterodont**, is generalized for the consumption of foods from many sources. Most species will favor some kinds of foods over others, but all will consume a variety of fruits, nuts, leaves, and other plants, in addition to some meat.

The primate mouth has four kinds of teeth—incisors, canines, premolars, and molars—as in most other mammals. Primate molars are low crowned, with blunt cusps for chewing. Primates have a reduced number of incisors and premolars when compared with other mammals. Primate canines and incisors are used for biting, pulling, and cutting. This dental formula makes primates highly adaptable to a variety of foods and capable of changing their eating habits quickly based on changes in their environment.

Skull, Brain, and Senses

Evolutionary changes in the primate skull and brain have generally favored the sense of vision over the sense of smell, particularly in diurnal species.

Binocular vision. Primate eyes have a forward orientation and provide stereoscopic vision. Having two eyes with overlapping fields of vision allows the brain to combine images that are only slightly different in their horizontal projection. The differences provide a sense of depth and dimensionality. The primate brain has developed special structures to interpret three-dimensionality and depends on both eyes transmitting overlapping images to the brain at the same time. Judging distance is especially important to tree-dwelling animals capable of jumping from branch to branch. The anatomy of the primate skull has several modifications to accommodate **binocular vision**. These include a shorter snout, a flatter face, and a bony ridge on the rear edge of the orbit that forms a protective

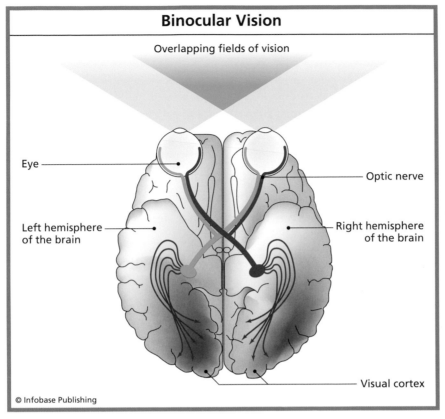

Binocular Vision

Overlapping fields of vision

Eye

Optic nerve

Left hemisphere
of the brain

Right hemisphere
of the brain

Visual cortex

© Infobase Publishing

Binocular vision. The fields of vision overlap and the optic signal for each
eye is detected by both hemispheres of the brain.

encasement for the eye called a postorbital bar. The latter feature
is more pronounced in the more advanced primates, including the
great apes and humans.

Diurnal primates have color vision, while **nocturnal** species—
those active mostly at night—do not.

Enlarged brain. Primates have a reduction in some senses when
compared with other mammals. For example, the primate senses of
smell and hearing are less acute than in many other kinds of mammals. Other portions of the primate brain have become enlarged
over the course of primate evolution, however, especially in regard
to the vision and cognitive centers. Larger brain capacity provides

increased intelligence and improved adaptability—key factors in the success of primates.

Reproduction and Life Cycle

The life cycle of primates is generally longer when compared with those of other mammals. Primates have an extended period of fetal gestation. Once born, primates mature quite slowly. Every aspect of growth seems to take longer in primates than in other mammals. From the gestation period, to the time spent being cared for as an infant, to the eruption of baby teeth followed by adult teeth, to the reaching of sexual maturity, primates exhibit prolonged life histories.

Most primate species usually have single offspring. This contrasts sharply with the many other, mostly small, mammals that routinely have multiple births. Instead of counting on sheer numbers to further the survival of the species, primates have adopted a strategy dependent on extended parental care and protection and longer life cycles to further their kind. In an important sense, primates use their greater intelligence to ensure the survival of their numbers. Having a longer life and a larger brain enables them to adapt continually and adjust to the dangers and risks of life. This provides primates with advantages beyond their genetically provided, innate adaptations.

BEHAVIORAL CHARACTERISTICS OF HIGHER PRIMATES

In addition to anatomical traits, there also are behavioral characteristics that distinguish haplorhine primates from other mammals. The study of primate behavior—one of the key subdisciplines of the field of **primatology**—opens a window onto the ways early humans may have acted, interacted, and survived. Behavior is also part of the fabric of the life events that contribute to the survival and adaptation of a species. As such, behavior is subject to the same forces of natural selection that govern the continuance of an individual and, ultimately, the population of which that individual is a member.

Because of the close relationship of nonhuman hominoids to humans, much fieldwork has been done in the study of the social behavior of such nonhuman hominoids as chimpanzees, orangutans, bonobos, and gorillas. The social behavior of these primates is the subject of this section.

Primate Social Behavior

Higher primates, including hominoids, are social animals, and they display a suite of unique social behaviors that contribute to their success and survival. The study of primate behavior is the work of primatologists. They do their work by observing captive animals in zoos or by studying free-ranging animals in their natural habitats. Each approach has certain advantages.

The observation of captive animals not only allows the primatologist to study the biology of living subjects but, perhaps more significantly, also provides an opportunity to interact with the species. This has been particularly important for the study of the communication skills of apes. Several historically important studies have shown that apes can be taught to communicate with humans through the use of such techniques as American Sign Language or images shown on a computer screen. In 1966, the husband-and-wife team of Beatrix T. Gardner (1933–2008) and R. Allen Gardner demonstrated that a young chimp could be taught to communicate using American Sign Language. This pioneering work led to many follow-up studies using a variety of communication methods.

The Gardners chose American Sign Language as their method of communicating with chimps because these apes lack vocal cords with the same kind of verbal acuity as found in humans. Another American researcher, Sue Savage-Rumbaugh of the Great Ape Trust, spent 30 years at Georgia State University perfecting techniques that included computer voice synthesis for communicating with great apes, including bonobos. Among her techniques, she used a computer keyboard and voice synthesis to allow the animals to "talk" using spoken English. Savage-Rumbaugh's research has done much to document the ability of apes to recognize and recall symbols, comprehend spoken words, decode language patterns, and learn basic concepts related to counting and quantity. Her work has added much to the understanding of the intelligence of these close relatives of humans.

Primatologists who study free-ranging populations of primates hope to observe their subjects in as natural a setting as possible. This means that the primates live in a habitat that is normally unaffected by the presence of humans. Researchers conduct fieldwork by living in close proximity to their subjects, a process that first requires a period of habituation, until the novelty of human presence reduces the natural fear and anxiety that the primate subjects might initially express. Only then, after perhaps many weeks of blending in with a given primate population, will a researcher begin to observe behavior that might closely resemble behavior that might occur if no human were present.

Without the dedication of such field workers, we would know little about the various social structures of the higher primates. American psychologist Robert Yerkes (1876–1956) was one of the first to conduct field studies of gorillas and chimpanzees. A pioneer of intelligence testing in the early 1900s, Yerkes became interested in the comparative study of the psychology of apes and humans. "Certainly it is unwise to assume that human biology can be advanced only by the study of man himself," wrote Yerkes in 1943. By the 1930s, Yerkes was sending students into the field to study gorillas and chimpanzees. Other landmarks in the field study of primates included Japanese field research begun in 1948 by Kinji Imanishi (1902–1992) and Junichiro Itani (1926–2001), who documented the social behavior of macaques, and the pioneering work of British primatologist Jane Goodall (b. 1934), who has studied free-ranging chimpanzees in Tanzania for more than 40 years.

The Advantages of Being Social

Among the primates, anthropoids are best known for their social behavior. Why does social behavior benefit the anthropoids? This is a complicated question because the nature and benefits of social behavior vary even within the affected primate social groups. One thing is certain: Living in social groups has benefited anthropoids for many thousands of years as a successful adaptive response to ecological factors that otherwise might have impeded their ability to survive as a species.

Living together has risks. It exposes individuals to competition for resources. Living in a social group also increases the likelihood of injury because of conflict with one's fellow group members. Being in a group also complicates mate selection; it can lead to rivalries, face-offs, and even death. Anthropoids have learned to accept these consequences of competition with their own kind to offset the larger risks of going it alone in a world full of even greater dangers.

One of the key advantages to living in a group is the natural protection from predators that a group offers. According to one hypothesis, anthropoids are more likely to avoid being preyed on because they live together in self-policing, vigilant groups. Higher primates are vulnerable to a range of small and large predators, ranging from snakes and birds to large cats and humans. Living in a group immediately reduces the likelihood of any one individual being preyed on to the exclusion of others. This safety-in-numbers strategy is found in many kinds of animals that live in large groups, from fish, to birds, to antelope. Living in groups also provides a collective awareness of the environment: Many eyes, noses, and ears are at the ready to detect the first signs of an approaching predator. When a predator is detected, it is common among nonhuman primates to let out a warning call. Baboons bark, chimpanzees scream, and lemurs hoot.

Another benefit of living in social groups is the acquisition and protection of food resources. Being omnivorous, anthropoids are able to consume many kinds of foods. Most species tend to favor one type of food over another, however, and may spend many waking hours foraging. Mountain gorillas subsist mainly on leaves. Chimpanzees are primarily fruit eaters but will supplement their diet when necessary with honey, termites, nuts, birds' eggs, and small mammals. Chimpanzees divide their time equally between eating and moving from one food-source location to the next.

Living in a social group leverages the talents of individuals with the most successful foraging skills. It also allows the group not only to acquire food but also to protect that food from other animals. Finding and eating food as a group does, however, introduce competition among group members, and the rank of an individual in the group will influence that individual's access to food.

Acquiring food and guarding against predation often are fused as primate groups go foraging. In the case of baboon troops—*troop* is the name given to a baboon social group—their food consists largely of roots, tubers, leaves, flowers, fruits, and small animals. All of these food sources normally are found on the ground. Large cats are a serious threat to a baboon troop, and a foraging group relies on its largest males to protect the group.

The Social Structures of Nonhuman Primates

Field studies of different species of higher primates reveal that these animals are self-organized, using a variety of social structures. These social patterns and hierarchies vary from species to species and sometimes vary even within a given species. Generally speaking, however, the following five social structures are recognized for nonhuman primates:

Bonded pair and offspring. This social structure consists of an adult female-male pair and all of that pair's offspring. The adults usually mate for life in this structure. In most cases, the offspring leave the unit when they reach sexual maturity.

Single female and her offspring. In some primate species, bonds are strongest between a female and her offspring, and the broader social organization is made up of multiple groups of single females and their respective young. Each single-female unit may occupy a specific area, called its home range; the ranges of multiple single-female units may overlap. In this social structure, interaction with males is limited except during mating,

COMPARING NONHUMAN ANTHROPOID SOCIAL GROUPS

Anthropoid Type	Characteristics
Gibbons and siamangs	Bonded pair and offspring; one adult male, one adult female, and their offspring; no other permanent social group
Orangutans	Single female and her offspring; no other permanent social group
Chimpanzees	Fission-fusion society; community whose members may separate from the larger group temporarily for purposes such as foraging; no permanent cohesive group; 10 to more than 100 members in a community
Bonobos	Fission-fusion society; community whose members may separate from the larger group temporarily for purposes such as foraging; no permanent cohesive group; strong females tend to lead; 15 to 150 members in a community
Gorillas	One (adult) male group, several females; 5 to 30 members in a community
Baboons	Troop; smaller, one-male group within community; females have strong bonds; males often transfer from one group to another; 10 to 200 members in a community

and the males tend to range over a wide area that encompasses the home ranges of several females.

Fission-fusion society. In this structure, a large overall social group breaks up on a regular basis into smaller groups that then will regroup to re-form the larger unit again. The breaking up into smaller groups is often associated with a task such as foraging. In bonobos, for example, the entire group may sleep together in one spot each night but divide and disperse into smaller foraging groups by day. The composition of these smaller groups may change from day to day.

One (adult) male group. In this form of social organization, one male is associated with multiple females and services them for mating purposes. Despite appearances, the male is not necessarily the determining factor in the formation and development of such a group. In some cases, it is the female who chooses to be in a one-male group, not the male who chooses the female. Among mountain gorillas, females sometimes may transfer among one-male groups. In some species of baboons, the bond between females is actually stronger than the bond between a male and his so-called harem.

Troop. In larger groups in which it becomes impractical for a single male to monopolize or defend a large number of females within his group, males will compete to gain first access. Females in such organizations tend to develop close bonds among themselves. Males, on reaching puberty, often will switch to another, neighboring group rather than continue to struggle for dominance against antagonizing male counterparts.

Other Characteristics of Higher Primate Behavior

Living in groups leads to a number of other innovative features of higher primate behavior. As social animals, primates have a natural dependency on others to perpetuate their own survival and that of the species.

Some primate societies have a dominance hierarchy in which individual males have a given status within the group. This is particularly true of baboons and chimpanzees. Those individuals who are dominant have more influence on the collective behavior of the group and on the choice of mating partners. The dominant male generally is one of the largest and healthiest members of the group. Once established, a dominant male baboon may maintain his rank for a long time. Other, lesser males may form an alliance with the dominant male and protect him from aggressive moves by newcomers to the troop. Changes eventually take place as dominant males grow old and weaken or die.

Female primates also establish hierarchies, and these are sometimes more important than male hierarchies within a social group. Among baboons, these hierarchies generally are based on the rank of a female's mother within the group. Females with infants often carry a special status within a group as well and often are guarded by other member of the social order. In bonobos, rank often is determined by female-to-female bonds as well as by bonds between a female and her male offspring. Bonobo males yield to females when feeding, and groups of females have been observed attacking males.

Many forms of communication are exhibited by all animals. These forms of communication include instinctive behaviors that convey emotions, express fear, or represent intent. Higher primates add to this repertoire of autonomic communicative responses a suite of purposeful, often learned behaviors that also serve as communication.

Primates engage in a large collection of verbal and nonverbal expressions, from vocalizations to gestures, facial expressions, and touching. Chimpanzees engage in prolonged eye contact as a mild threat. A more serious threat gesture might consist of a chimp exposing its large canine teeth, wobbling back and forth while crouching, or shaking the branches of a tree to intimidate another primate or intruder. Researchers have studied the facial expressions of chimpanzees closely; the expressions reveal a set of typical "faces" that now can be interpreted.

Although primates do not use verbal language the way humans do, they often have a wide range of vocalizations available to convey basic information to others of their kind. Such vocalizations might enable the primate to signal danger, to indicate the presence of food, to express anger, or even to express satisfaction to other members of its group.

Social groups are never without conflicts, resolutions, and amicable interactions between members. Aggressive behaviors such as fighting, biting, and chasing individuals away from food sources are not uncommon in primate societies. Behaviors that bring resolution and calm to the social group are known as *affiliative behaviors*. These behaviors often involve touching and friendly physical contact. Social grooming—in which one individual uses its fingers to pick dirt, insects, or other materials from the fur of another—is highly particular to primate species. Some primate species engage in this pleasurable activity for long periods.

Learning and Tools

Nonhuman anthropoids are also distinguished by their capacity for learning. In many ways they show an aptitude equal to that of humans for observing, imitating, and mastering tasks. The behavior of most organisms exists at an instinctive or autonomic level and is programmed by the organisms' genes. Anthropoids, however, are able to add to their repertory of inherited behaviors by learning new behaviors throughout their lives. This ability to learn and respond to obstacles in life's path provides anthropoids with a tremendous adaptive advantage.

Examples of anthropoid learning abound in the annals of field researchers. In 1979, while studying Japanese macaques, primatologist Michael Huffman of Kyoto University noticed a lone female monkey playing by herself with small rocks in a manner much like that of a child banging together and stacking a set of building blocks. On his return to the same locality in 1983, Huffman was astounded to see that half or more of the macaque troop was now engaged in stacking and banging stones, sometimes even on the roofs of local houses, creating quite a disturbance. Most interesting was that this behavior, apparently picked up and passed from monkey to monkey within the troop, had no obvious purpose other than self-amusement. During earlier studies of macaques, dating back to the 1950s, researchers had observed a young female monkey who began to wash dirt from sweet potatoes. This behavior then was learned by the young female's mother and slowly began to spread to other members of the troop. Infants copied the behavior quickly. After 10 years, three-quarters of the macaques had adopted the potato-washing behavior.

When such behaviors are passed along to other members of a group, a **culture** arises. "Culture and innovation are often ways of adapting to environmental changes, or a response to a change in lifestyle," explains Huffman. The ability of higher primates to learn greatly improves their ability to adapt to their world.

Such learned behavior is also related to toolmaking, one of the hallmarks of higher primate culture. Among free-ranging primates, only chimpanzees, orangutans, and capuchin monkeys are known to use tools. The capuchin monkey is a New World monkey from Central America. As such, it is only distantly related to the great apes—much more distantly related than are Old World monkeys. Yet no Old World monkey shows a capacity in the wild for tool-making. This leads researchers to assume that the ability to make tools was not inherited by a distant common ancestor of New World monkeys and anthropoids, but that it developed independently as an inherited trait in these different primate lineages. Humans, in turn, inherited the ability to make tools from their closest ancestors among the great apes.

Chimpanzees make and use a variety of tools in the wild. They sometimes strip sticks of leaves and insert the sticks into termite mounds to fish out the insects. Chimpanzees also are known to crush leaves into a spongelike wad to absorb water for drinking or to soak up termites. The variety of tools also may vary from one community of chimpanzees to another. In some cases, chimpanzees appear to use tools with an added degree of premeditation. In West Africa, chimpanzees have been seen using stones and rocks to crack open palm nuts. A chimpanzee will use one stone as an anvil-like base and then use the other to smash the nuts against the hard surface. Because no similar stones have been found in the immediate vicinity, it appears that the stones themselves are left near the palm trees by the chimpanzees for future use.

Variations of chimpanzee nut-cracking behaviors abound. Instead of rocks, some chimpanzee communities use the exposed root surfaces of hardwood trees as anvils. Furthermore, this behavior appears to have been adopted by generation after generation of chimpanzees. The animals have left behind traces of nut cracking that go back a few hundred years in some cases.

TOWARD THE HUMAN PRIMATE

Nonhuman primates provide a window on the kinds of adaptations and behaviors that were present in ancestral human species. Humans share many characteristics with catarrhine primates, especially the great apes. These characteristics include anatomical similarities related to diet, locomotion, reproduction, and larger brains. These nonhuman primates also demonstrate a variety of behaviors that also are found in humans, with social organization, communication, learning, and toolmaking being among the most fundamental.

A basic definition of culture requires that a population have a body of learned behaviors that are passed along to other members and generations of the society. By this definition, some species of great apes, including chimpanzees, possess actual cultures—a phenomenon that until about 50 years ago was thought to be exclusively human in origin. Today's field researchers not only assume that primates can have cultures but also now conduct comparative studies of different populations of the same species to detect cultural differences between them. Although human culture is vastly more complex than nonhuman primate culture, the study of nonhuman primate culture provides a vast resource for understanding the evolution of culture in our earliest ancestors.

SUMMARY

This chapter explored primate biology and behavior.

1. Humans are one of more than 200 kinds of living primates in the world today. Primates ("of the first") include the biological group made up of all lemurs, monkeys, and apes.
2. One of the most familiar and defining anatomical structures of primates is the grasping hand and, in some cases, the grasping foot.
3. Primate locomotion strategies comprise vertical clinging and leaping, brachiation in prosimians and Old World monkeys, and hanging and climbing in the apes. Most primates other than humans are quadrupedal (walking on all fours) when on the ground.
4. There is a strong tendency toward omnivory in primates, and their tooth pattern, although heterodont, is generalized for the consumption of many food sources.

5. Primates have large brains and binocular vision. Evolutionary changes in the primate skull and brain generally have favored the sense of vision over the sense of smell, particularly in diurnal species.

6. The life cycle of primates generally is longer when compared with other mammals. Most primate species usually have single offspring.

7. Behavior is subject to the same forces of natural selection that act on biological traits.

8. Living in social groups has benefited anthropoids for many thousands of years and has furthered their survival.

9. Living in groups has many benefits, including protection from predators and the acquisition and protection of food resources.

10. Field studies of different species of higher primates reveal that they are self-organized, using a variety of social structures.

11. Primates engage in a large collection of verbal and nonverbal expressions, from vocalizations to gestures, facial expressions, and touching.

12. Higher primates are good learners and are adept at using tools.

SECTION THREE:
Evolution of the Early Hominins

5

The Ape-Hominin Transition

The line of higher primates known as the Hominidae includes two subgroups: the apes (gibbons, orangutans, gorillas, chimpanzees, and bonobos) and humans. Humans and apes are linked by a common ancestor. Current fossil and genetic evidence shows that apes arose about 20 million to 25 million years ago in Africa, Turkey, and eastern Europe and diversified into numerous lineages that spread throughout the Old World. Paleontologists Peter Andrews of the Natural History Museum, London, and Jay Kelley of the University of Illinois use fossil remains of plants and apes from eastern Europe and Africa to explain a likely migration scenario for early hominoids.

The earliest apes, such as *Proconsul* and *Rangwapithecus* (earlier Miocene, Africa) from East Africa, were forest adapted. They lived an arboreal lifestyle in a multistoried, evergreen rainforest habitat. Plant fossils associated with apes that lived toward the middle part of the Miocene of East Africa suggest that the apes' woodland habitat had become more seasonal and was quite similar to the environment that existed at the same time in the more northerly Turkey. Andrews and Kelley proposed that as environments in Africa and eastern Europe shifted toward a more seasonal woodland habitat, apes were able to emigrate successfully to the north for much of the middle part of the Miocene. This migration occurred about 17 million years ago, while Europe and Africa still were largely joined, prior to the expansion of the Mediterranean Sea.

It was during the middle part of the Miocene Epoch that apes enjoyed their greatest diversity. Of approximately 33 known genera of living and fossil hominoids, 28 are extinct, and 24 of those lived during the Miocene.

By the end of the Miocene, as the lineages of apes diminished, they also diverged onto two evolutionary paths. One path split off between 13 million and 15 million years ago and led to orangutans. The other path led to modern African apes and eventually to humans, which split from the lineage of *Pan* (the chimpanzee) between 5 million and 7 million years ago. One recent study of the chimpanzee genome by a team of scientists from Harvard and the Massachusetts Institute of Technology concluded that the speciation of humans took place no later than 6.3 million years ago.

Recent molecular studies of anthropoid genetic evolution have led to a change in the terminology used to describe humans and their most immediate ancestors. The term *hominid* previously was used to include all orangutans, gorillas, chimpanzees, and humans. Recent gene studies have revealed, however, that orangutans split from the great ape line earlier than was once thought. This means that humans, gorillas, and chimpanzees are more closely related to one another than they are to orangutans. For the purpose of classification, the hominoids were divided into two subgroups: the Ponginae (orangutans) and the Homininae (gorillas, chimpanzees, humans and their ancestors). Furthermore, the term *Hominini* is reserved exclusively for humans and ancestral humans since the time of their divergence from other great apes. As a result, humans and their ancestors now are referred to as hominins instead of hominids. Within this book, the term *human* is used to refer to any species of the genus *Homo*, or modern humans. Hominin species prior to *Homo* also are referred to as *ancestral humans*.

This chapter explores this pivotal time in the evolution of humans, the so-called ape-hominin transition during which ancestral humans first arose.

BECOMING HUMAN

We already have seen that many of the anatomical and behavioral traits found in humans are also characteristic of other primates, especially the hominoids. Large brains, social living, a long gestation period and extended childhood, and the use of tools and language all are characteristics found to some degree in both nonhuman primates and humans. The publication, in 2005, of the chimpanzee genome by a research group known as the Chimpanzee Sequencing and Analysis Consortium revealed that the genetic makeup of humans is only 2.7 percent different from that of chimps, our closest relatives among the great apes. This statistically small difference in the genetic makeup of human and chimpanzees leads naturally to the question of what makes us human.

Fortunately, the patchy but revealing record of early hominin fossils provides paleontologists with compelling specimens that can be studied and compared. In piecing these clues together, the stages of evolution that lead to anatomically modern humans—*Homo sapiens*—can be seen as a story of increasingly derived traits for specializations such as locomotion, food consumption, and the broadening application of intelligence. There was not, however, a single path that led to modern humans. The notion of a "missing link" between modern humans and extinct apes remains fixed in popular culture, but science long ago realized that there were many divergent evolutionary paths leading to modern humans.

Apes and hominins most certainly have a common ancestor in the form of an extinct species of primate. The known fossil clues to ancestral humans do not, however, link neatly together as a single progression of evolutionary steps resulting in modern humans. As anthropologist Conrad Kottak points out, "Humans are not descended from gorillas or chimps. Rather, humans and the African apes share a common ancestor—a creature that was like chimps and gorillas in some ways, like humans in others." Each group of apes evolved along divergent paths, and many species have since become extinct, including those of some ancestral hominins. We might think of the human family tree as a collection of fallen twigs without the tree. Although all of the twigs stemmed from the same ancient roots, the branches that once connected the twigs to the trunk have been lost in time. A diagram showing the phylogeny of hominin evolution consists of the known scraps of independently evolving lineages, often overlapping but not developing identically.

The human ancestry diagram identifies ancestral human species that range from the time of early human speciation in the late Miocene Epoch, between 5 million and 7 million years ago; through the appearance of multiple ancestral humans; and finally to the genus *Homo* in the latest part of the Pliocene Epoch. This view of human evolution naturally sheds light on the many extinct forms of humans that existed before today. It was not until recently that *Homo sapiens* existed alone as the only species of hominin. For most of the more than 2 million years of *Homo* existence, there were several other diverse and long-existing *Homo* species. At least six species of *Homo* currently are recognized. In addition to *Homo*, there were 10 to 12 other hominin species, some of which overlapped in time with the earliest *Homo* species.

A suite of anatomical features separates hominins from other anthropoids. Physical evidence from the fossil record provides many clues to the emergence of these traits. Among the evidence is a suite of changes that led to **bipedalism**—walking upright on two legs—as well as to larger brains and modification to the teeth and jaws.

Bipedal Primates

One of the key distinguishing features of hominins is bipedalism. Indeed, obligate bipedalism—where no other form of locomotion is practical—might have been the first uniquely human adaptation to distinguish hominins from other anthropoids. Paleoanthropologist Milford H. Wolpoff (b. 1942) suggests two advantages underlying human bipedalism. First, by dedicating the **hind limbs** alone to locomotion, the forelimbs (hands and arms) are freed for other tasks such as carrying tools and food and otherwise interacting with the environment.

A second advantage is that hominin locomotion is more efficient than other primate locomotion. In the case of long-distance walking, for example, a bipedal hominin can cover comparatively great distances while expending only a fraction of the energy required by an anthropoid walking on all fours. This energy efficiency reduces

The African landscape of the Miocene Epoch began a changeover from a predominantly forested habitat to one in which grassy plains became more widespread.

body heat, increases stamina, and allows a hominin to extend its manageable range to a broad geographic territory. As discussed below, a number of anatomical changes contribute to the efficiency of bipedal living.

Environmental changes may have influenced the adaptation of bipedalism. Geologic and climatic changes during the late Miocene Epoch produced a drier world. In East Africa, the possible cradle of hominin evolution, grasslands expanded and tropical rain forests receded. These changes provided a habitat of new, open vistas for primates to explore. Bipedalism may have provided advantages for crossing such expanses, for scanning the horizon for predators or prey, and for retreating to the forest at night to gain refuge in trees.

Kottak points out that early hominins were still partly arboreal and could have found safety from nocturnal predators by sleeping at night in trees.

The table that follows summarizes some of the factors that may have influenced the evolution of bipedal locomotion in hominins.

African apes are not the ideal models to use when trying to picture the kind of primate from which hominins evolved. Wolpoff points out that because certain derived features in humans, such as the shortening of the lower back, are not present in gorillas and chimpanzees, such features must have been inherited from an earlier human ancestor. Among the skeletal adaptations that developed to support bipedalism were the following.

Skull and vertebral column. The point of connection at which the skull meets the vertebral column is called the **foramen magnum.** It is a hole in the bony base of the skull. In apes, the foramen

FACTORS INFLUENCING THE EVOLUTION OF BIPEDAL LOCOMOTION IN HOMININS*

Factor	Hypotheses
Carrying objects	Bipedal posture freed the hands to carry objects such as weapons, provisions, and offspring.
Hunting	Carrying a weapon made hunting more effective.
Seed and nut gathering and feeding	Standing upright and using the hands to gather seeds, nuts, and berries provided access to food in the higher branches of bushes and the lower branches of trees.
Thermoregulation	Standing upright allowed the body to cool more easily by exposing less surface area directly to the midday sun and providing immersion in cooler breezes above the ground surface.
Visual surveillance	Being upright provided a better view of the surroundings, making it easier to spot predators, food resources, and other members of one's group.
Long-distance walking	Bipedalism provided a physiologically more efficient means of covering long distances, thereby extending the range of food gathering.

*Based on Jurmain, Kilgore, and Trevathan, *Introduction to Physical Anthropology*, tenth edition, 2005

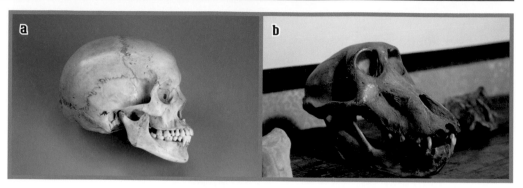

The skull of a human (*left*) and a great ape (*right*)

magnum is positioned on the back of the skull, with neck muscles also running to the rear of the skull. In hominins, the foramen magnum is beneath the skull, positioned in such a way that the spine connects from beneath. Hominin neck muscles are below the skull. The head of the biped—the hominin—is therefore balanced on top of the spine and requires less neck musculature than does the head of the ape, whose head is positioned out in front of the spine. The hominin spine also has a more pronounced S-curve shape than does the spine of an ape. This keeps the hominin body centered above the pelvis for balance.

Pelvis. Unlike quadrupeds, bipeds place most of their weight on one leg as they move. To make this sort of gait work without losing balance, a biped's skeleton must continually shift the center of gravity from one leg to the other. Primates with nonobligate bipedalism, such as chimps, remain balanced on two legs by walking in a rocking fashion to shift their entire weight from one leg to the other. In contrast to the more compressed hip of a chimp, the hominin hip is broader and bowl-like and supports the weight of internal organs. This lowers the center of gravity of the hominin body. At the same time, a suite of muscle attachments on the hip provide balance even when the hominin is standing on one leg, shifting muscle power to accommodate the center of gravity without needing to shift the

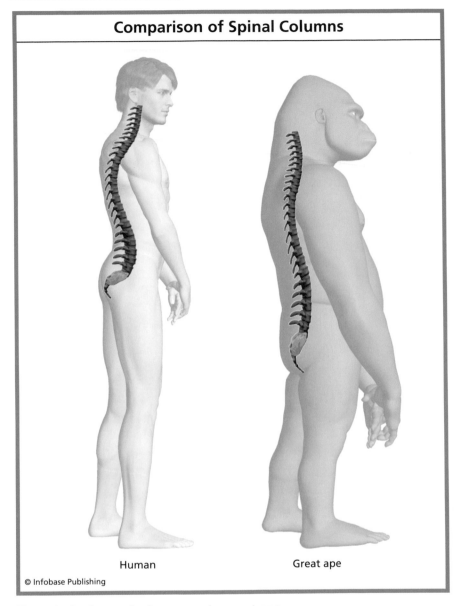

Comparison of Spinal Columns

Human

Great ape

© Infobase Publishing

The spinal column of a human and a great ape

entire body from side to side as does a chimp. A related consequence of pelvic structure is the size allotted for the hominin birth canal. This adaptation of a pelvis for better balance also narrows the birth canal. This narrowed birth canal was a possible obstacle to the development of the hominin skull and brain, a factor that apparently has been compensated for by a longer period of childhood development, during which the skull and brain grow dramatically once outside the mother's womb.

Leg. To position the legs below the hips, the upper leg bone, or **femur**, of the hominin is angled downward at the point at which it connect to the pelvis. The **tibia**—the lower leg bone—is longer than in other anthropoids and is angled inward to improve balance by keeping the legs positioned under the body. Adaptations to the knee joint between the femur and the tibia provide a wide range of flexibility so that the legs can easily be folded inward or fully straightened.

Foot. In the hominin foot, the big toe is much larger than the other toes and is brought into line with them. This contrasts with the grasping morphology of the feet of apes. The hominin foot also developed an arch, not seen in apes, to absorb shock through a heel-down, toes-off walking motion. By absorbing shock, the arches of hominins' feet help reduce fatigue and even prevent the fracturing of the lower leg bones.

The anatomical features of bipedalism just outlined represent the more derived form of upright walking found in anatomically modern humans. These aspects of bipedalism were not all present to the same degree in ancestral humans, as will be seen in the discussion of specific hominin fossil species later in this chapter.

Teeth and Jaws

In the search for early hominins, the availability of tooth specimens has been particularly important in detecting the transitional stages that separated hominins from apes.

The generalized tooth battery of the great apes is characterized by large, pointed canine teeth and a U-shaped jaw pattern in which the teeth located behind the canines are lined up in two parallel rows. In the upper jaw of a great ape there is a gap—known as a diastema—between the upper canines and the incisors. In

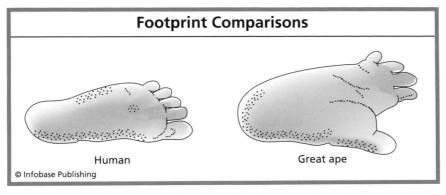

Footprint Comparisons

Human

Great ape

© Infobase Publishing

Comparison of the left foot of a human (*left*) and great ape (*right*).
This shows the contrast in the oblique axis (OA) at the digit joints and
transverse axis (TA) between the big toe and joint of the second digit.

the lower jaw, there is a corresponding gap between the lower canines and the first premolars. These gaps provide a space for the oversized canine teeth when an ape's jaws are closed. Apes use their large canine teeth to pierce fruit, to intimidate others, and to defend themselves.

A general pattern in the reduction of the size of the teeth can be seen in human evolution. The canines of hominins are greatly reduced when compared with those of apes and functionally are no different from the incisors. Hominin canine teeth, like hominin incisors, are used to grip and tear rather than to puncture and slice as in apes. The diastemas seen in the jaws of apes also are missing in later hominins because of the reduction of the canines and the development of a different chewing process. Rather than being severely U-shaped as in apes, the hominin jaw is gently parabolic, with many grinding surfaces.

Whereas the ape jaw is adapted for cutting and slashing food, the hominin jaw and teeth evolved to maximize chewing and grinding capability. In hominins, the front teeth (incisors and canines) became reduced and so became better adapted for plucking and tearing. Molars, although still quite large in early hominins, also became reduced and developed thick tooth enamel to improve their grinding capability. Generally speaking, hominin teeth have been adapted to provide a strong, evenly distributed biting force that can be sustained for a long time. This adaptation coincided with changes in the world of the early hominins. That world consisted of broad grasslands in which the vegetation was tough and fibrous. The chewing adaptations of hominins were maximized by a gradual repositioning of the jaw muscles so that they favored the back teeth. In apes, the jaw muscles favor the front teeth.

Brain Size and Organization

Intelligence is another characteristic that separates hominins from the great apes. The intellectual capacities of hominins represent some of their most astounding adaptations. Intelligence may be defined as the use of the brain to respond to, process, and act on information. This involves the detection of sensory input—sounds, sights, touches, tastes, and smells—and the operation of a network of nerve connections throughout the body that channel that sensory input to the brain for interpretation.

To some extent, these characteristics of intelligence are present in most animals. Animal behavior specialist Donald R. Griffin (1915–2003) applied a basic definition of consciousness to animals other than humans, based largely on his study of the behavior of many kinds of animals in their free-ranging habitats. "Animal thoughts and emotions presumably concern matters of immediate importance to the animals themselves, rather than kinds of conscious thinking that are primarily relevant to human affairs," wrote Griffin in his 1992 book *Animal Minds*. In that book, Griffin identified the following traits of consciousness that are shared by humans and other animals:

- Humans and other animals have anatomical similarities in the **neural** function of the brain.
- Humans and other animals consistently modify their behaviors in adaptive ways.
- The complexity of a given animal's mental capacity is reflected by an equally complex method of communication.

Human intellect goes beyond the mere reflexive response to external stimuli and poses other definitional challenges. Finding a cause for the explosion of intelligence that is found in the species *Homo* also poses challenges.

Living socially is perhaps one driving force behind hominin intellectual evolution. Writing in 1990, biologist Richard D. Alexander of the University of Michigan suggested that natural selection acted on the evolution of the hominin brain because of the social context in which hominins developed. Basing his premise on earlier work (1976) by psychologist Nicholas K. Humphrey, then of Cambridge University, Alexander suggested that "the human intellect evolved as a means of dealing with the uncertainties of social life." Putting it another way, high levels of cooperation within hominin social groups, as well as high levels of competition and dysfunction, were central, Alexander said, "in creating the environment of brain and psyche selection." Those hominins who succeeded in their social discourse also succeeded in furthering their lineage and inheritable traits related to brain function and capacity. Alexander proposed three elements of human consciousness: self-awareness, the ability to imagine possible alternatives, and the capacity to interpret the mental state of others.

As the hominin brain evolved, it grew bigger, and its neural connections reorganized to handle more complex processing functions. Although modern technology such as magnetic resonance imaging (MRI) can aid scientists who study the way the brain works in living individuals, paleontologists must turn to fossil evidence to ascertain how and when the hominin brain changed in ancestral humans. Even though the brain itself is never fossilized, its size, shape, and neural connections can be determined by making an endocast of the braincase. An endocast is a cast made of the brain cavity inside the skull. Such a cast not only indicates the general shape and organization of a brain, but also reveals the impressions made on the skull walls by the outside surface of the brain. This information can reveal much about the sizes, shapes, organization, and capacities of the brains of extinct creatures.

You sometimes hear about people being "right-brained" or "left-brained." This idea stems from the fact that the human brain is divided into two distinct halves, each of which is dedicated to certain functions. A "right-brained" person often is thought of as being visual or creative because that side of the brain is responsible for understanding spatial relationships and visualizing complex patterns. A "left-brained" person often is characterized as being highly logical or analytical. These descriptions of human traits are based on simplifications of descriptions of aspects of the organization of the human brain.

The mammal brain has three main parts. The brain stem is at the base of the brain and connects the brain directly to the spinal cord. The brain stem serves as a conduit for the neural signals that pass back and forth between the brain and the rest of the body. The brain stem also controls many automatic body functions such as those of the cardiovascular system, respiration, sensitivity to pain, consciousness, and sleep regulation.

The cerebellum ("little brain") is packed in at the base of the brain, behind the brain stem. The cerebellum is responsible for regulating voluntary muscle movement, balance, and posture.

The cerebrum is the largest part of the brain. It is the part that we visualize most clearly when we think of the brain. The cerebrum is divided into two halves, or hemispheres. Each hemisphere is devoted to a different suite of higher brain functions such as language, analysis, and the senses. The two hemispheres are joined by a thick bundle of nerve fibers called the *corpus callosum*. The *corpus callosum* enables the two halves of the cerebrum to work together and also permits them to work separately for certain functions. The concept of right brain and left brain originates with this basic anatomical feature of the cerebrum.

Endocasts of hominin brains show that the most obvious changes in the size and organization of the brain have taken place in the cerebrum. In most mammals, the two hemispheres of the brain are not divided to handle different functions but actually mirror each other. Memories, for example, are stored twice. In computer terms, the brains of nonhuman mammals consist of redundant systems to provide backup and uninterrupted performance in case of injury. Milford H. Wolpoff describes this advantage as allowing normal functions to continue even if part of the brain is damaged.

What, however, would happen if this redundancy were to be eliminated in favor of using the other, redundant half of the brain for additional functions? This, apparently, is how hominins managed to evolve additional and often novel higher brain functions while still managing to cram all of these capabilities into a relatively compact skull. The loss of redundancy, especially in memory capacity, might seem like a severe trade-off, but Wolpoff points out that "culture has largely taken the place of redundant information storage." Why store information in the brain if you can use language and writing to store it on the outside?

The accompanying table summarizes which functions of the human brain are found in which hemispheres.

The brain is, of course, more than just a bundle of nerves. To fully understand the intelligence of another creature, one must be able to observe a living specimen. Because this is not possible in the study of fossil humans, researchers have devised a relative measure of brain function called the **encephalization quotient** (EQ). Also known as a brain-to-body-mass ratio, the EQ is a ratio that compares the actual brain mass of an animal with the expected brain mass of an animal of that size. Larger animals obviously have larger brains, so brain size alone does not provide a reliable measure for intelligence. The development of such a quotient provided an objective, measurable way to determine the potential for intelligence in an animal even when working with only an endocast of a fossil skull.

An EQ of 1.0—a measure based on the anatomy of the common house cat—is used to indicate a normal brain size for an animal of a given size. An EQ higher than 1.0 indicates a brain that is bigger than expected for a mammal of the same size. An EQ less than 1.0 suggests a brain that is smaller than expected.

SOME HEMISPHERIC DIFFERENCES
IN HUMAN BRAIN FUNCTION

Left (dominant) hemisphere	Right (nondominant) hemisphere
Auditory	**Auditory**
Speech sounds	Melody recognition
Processing of consonant syllables	Vocal nonspeech sounds (coughing, laughing, crying)
Symbol translation and analysis	Steady-state vowels
Language production centers	
Recall of auditory images of visual objects	
Visual	**Visual**
Perceptual recognition of conceptual similarity	Drawing, building models from a picture
Naming items perceived	Two- and three-dimensional space relations Perceptual recognition of identity
Tactile and Motor	**Tactile and Motor**
Localization and naming of body parts	Contralateral motor control
Contralateral motor control	Tactile pattern recognition
Fine-hand motor skills	Awareness of illness
Hand gestures during speech	
Conceptual	**Conceptual**
Short-term memory	"Gestalt-synthetic" operations on perceptual material
Right-left differentiation	Spatial mapping
"Logical-analytical" operations on perceptual material	
Semantic mapping	
Temporal sequential ordering	

Source: Adapted from Laughlin and d'Aquili (1974), Kolb and Whishaw (1985), and Wallace (1992)

Comparing the EQs of different mammal species quickly puts this ratio into perspective, but such comparison also has its drawbacks. Based on an EQ of 1.0 for a cat, an opossum has an EQ of 0.4; a caribou, 0.78; a chimpanzee, 2.38; a dolphin, 6.0; and a *Homo sapiens*, 6.28. Generally speaking, primates deviate from the ratios expected in other mammals. This means that primates have relatively large brains for the size of their bodies. A word of caution is in order about these figures, however. EQ calculations vary widely from researcher to researcher, based on each researcher's own methods of estimating cranial capacity, brain mass, and body weight. Two of the leading researchers, Harry Jerison (University of California) and Robert Martin (The Field Museum), use formulas that produce results that can differ by as much as 28 percent from the calculations of other researchers when used to calculate EQ for hominins.

The EQ formula also is biased toward smaller animals and so loses it relevancy when used to examine animals of enormous size, especially whales. Also, in some mammals, including most primates, males have larger brains than females. However, given differences in body size, the EQ of males and females of a given species are usually about the same. Such is the case for orangutans, gorillas, and humans. Finally, because the EQ is based on brain size as well as body size, the forces of natural selection that act on the size of a mammal's body may be extreme without having much effect on an animal's relative intelligence when compared with individuals of different sizes of its own species. Craig Stanford points out that even though a German shepherd dog is much larger than a chihuahua, one would not say that the larger dog is any more intelligent than the smaller one.

Given these limitations of EQ as a way of comparing the intelligence of animals, it is perhaps best to think of EQ as a measure of the capacity for intelligence in a species rather than as a measure of a specific kind or expression of intelligence. As a measure of brain capacity, EQ can be especially helpful when used to compare changes seen in the evolution of a given lineage of related animals, including hominins.

The enlargement of the hominin brain closely followed the advent of bipedal locomotion. The fossil record of ancestral humans, represented primarily by the group known as **australopithecines** (described below), shows that their cranial capacity remained almost the same—from 400 to 530 cubic centimeters (cc)—for 2 million years. From an EQ standpoint, australopithecines were about as smart as modern gorillas, with a ratio between 1.87 and 2.50. With the coming of various *Homo* species, brain capacity expanded dramatically, from about 630 cc 2 million years ago to about 1,400 cc by about 300,000 years ago. The brain capacity of hominins has increased by about 400 percent over the past 3.5 million years. The table that follows compares the average cranial capacities and EQs of fossil hominins.

The rapid evolution of the size of the hominin brain is certainly the most remarkable aspect of human evolution. The reasons for the accelerated evolution of the brain are the source of much disagreement among paleoanthropologists. Because brain size is directly related to increased energy needs, the hominin brain would not have enlarged had there not been an advantage to its doing so. One explanation is that hominin brains increased in size and complexity because of the

AVERAGE CRANIAL CAPACITIES FOR FOSSIL HOMINIDS (ADULT SPECIMENS ONLY)

Taxon	Number of Specimens	Average Cranial Capacity (CC)	Range (CC)	Estimated EQ
A. afarensis	2	450	400–500	1.87
A. africanus	7	445	405–500	2.16
A. robustus and A. boisei	7	507	475–530	2.50
H. habilis	7	631	509–775	2.73–3.38
H. erectus	22	1,003	650–1,251	3.27
Archaic H. sapiens	18	1,330	1,100–1,586	3.52
H. neanderthalensis	19	1,445	1,200–1,750	4.04
Modern H. sapiens (older than 8,000 years)	11	1,490	1,290–1,600	5.27

Sources: Aiello and Dean (1990), Kappelman (1996), and Holloway (1999).
Note: Estimated EQs are not derived using all the specimens included in the second column.

demands of living in social groups in which interactions, conflicts, competition, and bonds occupied much of the time of each individual in a given group. That is to say, the stresses associated with living in complex social groups favor the natural selection of cognitive abilities that enable individuals to survive among others.

The role of nutrition and diet has been suggested as another factor in the rapid evolution of hominin brain size. In 1999, Craig Stanford suggested that meat eating among early humans provided a diet rich in protein and fats that supported the metabolic demands of increasingly large brains. Anthropologist William Leonard of Northwestern University assessed the energy needs of the modern human brain and compared those needs with the kinds of nutritional sources available to early hominins. What he found was that at rest, human brain **metabolism** accounts for 20 percent to 25 percent of an individual's total energy needs. This is far more than the 8 percent to 10 percent energy needs found in nonhuman primates.

Using this data on modern humans as a reference point, Leonard examined the brain-to-body-mass ratios of ancestral humans and determined that australopithecines (brain capacity of 450 cc) would have devoted about 11 percent of their resting energy to the brain. Early *Homo* species (brain capacity of 900 cc) would have allocated about 17 percent of their resting energy to the brain. Leonard concludes that early hominins could not have supported the energy requirements of such a hungry brain without having adopted a diet that was increasingly rich in calories and nutrients. While some of these additional calories certainly came from the consumption of meat, the evolution of the hominin jaw also shows that ancestral humans developed teeth and jaws that were increasingly adept at chewing a variety of vegetation, from leaves and fibrous stalks to fruits, nuts, and berries. All of this food went to feed the demands of an increasingly hungry brain.

SUMMARY

This chapter explored the evolution of early hominins and the traits that separated hominins from other apes.

1. Of approximately 33 known genera of living and fossil hominoids, 28 are extinct; 24 of those extinct genera lived during the Miocene.

2. Fossil evidence supports the hypotheses that chimpanzees, apes, and humans share a common ancestor that is more recent among this group than any common ancestor shared with organgutans.

3. The stages of evolution leading to *Homo sapiens* can be seen as a story of increasingly derived traits for specializations such as locomotion, food consumption, and the broadening application of intelligence.

4. Ancestral human species first appeared between 5 million and 7 million years ago.

5. At least six species of *Homo* are currently recognized. Existing prior to and overlapping with the evolution of *Homo* species were about 10 to 12 other hominin species.

6. The evolutionary links between ancestral hominin species are not well understood.

7. Distinguishing anatomical features of hominins include bipedalism; a general reduction in the size of dentition along with a jaw structure that favored the grinding of food using the back teeth; and an enlargement of the brain and associated gains in intelligence.

8. EQ is a mathematical formula for determining the capacity for intelligence based on a ratio of expected brain size to body size. The brain capacity of hominins has increased by about 400 percent over the past 3.5 million years.

6

THE EARLIEST
HUMAN ANCESTORS

Fossil clues to the existence of possible early hominins can be found in rocks that date from between 5 million and 7 million years ago, in the late Miocene Epoch. The fossil record for early humans is more complete during the early Pliocene Epoch, when there appears to have been a dramatic radiation of early hominin species throughout East Africa. In the search for early hominins, paleontologists look for fossils that include any of the telltale signs associated with the human species, as described in Chapter 5. These signs include evidence of bipedal locomotion, modified dental batteries with reduced canines and a thickening of tooth enamel on the molars, and skull and brain capacity, among others. This chapter explores the fossil evidence for early hominin species prior to *Homo*. The emergence of *Homo* is explored in *Early Humans*, another book in this series.

OUT OF AFRICA: EARLY HOMININS

Fossils representing the earliest examples of hominin species have been found in East Africa and date from about 5 million years ago, perhaps earlier. A few specimens from even earlier times, dating from between 5 million and 7 million years ago, may represent early hominins, but the fragmentary nature of these remains still leaves some doubt about this designation. The best-represented hominin species prior to *Homo* include those of *Australopithecus* ("southern ape"). *Australopithecus* is known from six undisputed species that ranged widely in East Africa from about 4.2 million to 1 million years ago.

Identifying early hominins from fragmentary remains is difficult because of the close resemblance of early hominins to apes. Without such telltale skeletal remains as a hip, foot, skull, jaw, or teeth, paleontologists are left with pieces of a jigsaw puzzle but no clear picture to which they can match those pieces. The fossil record is most spotty during the span of 5 million to 7 million years ago, when hominins first evolved as species distinct from the great apes. A little later, between 2 million and 4 million years ago, the fossil record is much clearer, and a fairly complete picture of early hominins can be surmised with accuracy. Researchers continue to comb the fossil beds of East Africa for more specimens, and each new one brings new revelations. There is promise that the gaps eventually will be filled and that the transition from apes to hominins will be more clearly spelled out in the future.

The first significant early hominin specimen was found in South Africa in 1925 and described by Raymond Dart (1893–1988), an Australian anatomist. Discovered in a limestone quarry in the small town of Taung, the fossil consisted of a small skull that Dart painstakingly extracted from the tough, rocky matrix in which it was sealed. The result was a lovely specimen of a juvenile skull. Dart had reason to believe that he was holding something more than the skull of an ape child. The specimen lacked the large canine teeth of apes, and its foramen magnum was positioned underneath the skull instead of at the **posterior**, indicating an upright posture. The specimen was popularly known as the "Taung child" because of its small size, but Dart gave it the scientific name of *Australopithecus africanus* ("southern ape of Africa"). Dart described the specimen, which was between 2.4 million and 3 million years old, as a transitional stage between apes and humans. The genus *Australopithecus* is now considered a hominin and was the first of its kind to be described.

Following the initial discoveries in South Africa, the search for early hominins broadened to East Africa. East Africa has produced

The Olduvai Gorge in the Great Rift Valley of East Africa

many extraordinary hominin specimens from a geologically rugged area known as the Great Rift Valley.

Located in the eastern Serengeti Plain of northern Tanzania, the Olduvai Gorge is one of the most important fossil-bearing regions of the Great Rift Valley. The gorge is about 30 miles long and consists of a deeply cut ravine in a mile-high grassy plateau. The semiarid climate, similar to that which probably existed when early hominins first lived there, makes the region hot, dry, and devoid of thick vegetation. These conditions are helpful in making visible the fossils that have eroded to the surface.

Another reason that the gorge is so accommodating to fossil hunters is that it exposes sedimentary layers that otherwise would not be accessible from the surface. The sedimentary layers also are easy to study, a factor that has led to excellent documentation about the ages of the various visible strata. Any fossils found in the region can be clearly dated and correlated with other specimens found in slightly different levels.

The first significant anthropological work in the Olduvai Gorge was conducted by Kenyan Louis Leakey and his British-born wife, Mary Leakey. Born of missionary parents in British East Africa (now Kenya), Louis met Mary, an anthropologist, while they were both doing field work in England. They married and moved to Kenya in 1937, had three children, and began to explore the Olduvai Gorge for fossils of human ancestors. The Leakeys' son Richard (b. 1944) and Richard's wife, Meave (b. 1942), also became noted fossil hunters. Together, for more than 40 years, this "first family" of anthropology has been at the center of discovery of early hominins. The family's work naturally attracted other researchers to the area, and although some of the work now has shifted to other areas of East Africa, the Leakeys and their pioneering work remain a profound influence on the science of early hominins.

The accompanying box summarizes the kinds of anatomical traits that enable paleontologists to distinguish fossil hominins from fossil apes.

A SURVEY OF FOSSIL HOMININS

A pivotal point in time in the speciation of ancestral humans was around 5 million years ago, at what today is known as the end of the Miocene Epoch and the beginning of the Pliocene. By the early Pliocene, human ancestors were ranging widely across Africa and establishing themselves as a species with some uniquely hominin characteristics. These characteristics included bipedalism and increasingly advanced intelligence. Prior to the 5 million-year marker, hominins were most certainly divesting themselves of their ancestral ape traits, perfecting bipedalism, and adapting to a rapidly changing African environment.

The following discussion is organized roughly chronologically, from the most primitive hominins to those that were possibly the direct ancestors of *Homo*.

Because there are numerous important species of the major genera of ancestral humans, the descriptions that follow are provided at the species level. The scientific names provided for these hominins include both the generic and species names, such as *Ardipithecus* (genus) *ramidus* (species). In discussing different species of the same genus, it is also a convention to abbreviate the genus name by signifying it with a capital letter alone, as in *A. afarensis* for *Australopithecus afarensis*.

ANATOMICAL TRAITS OF EARLY HOMININS

Features of the Skull

- reduced teeth overall, especially the canines
- reduced shearing mechanism between the upper canine and lower premolar when the jaw was closed
- molars with thick enamel
- rounded, parabolically shaped dental battery
- foramen magnum, the point of connection where the skull meets the vertebral column, positioned below the skull

Other Skeletal Features

- modifications to enable bipedalism, including:
  - broad, bowl-like pelvis
  - angled connection of the femur to the hip
  - arched feet
  - big toe aligned with other toes for balance
  - flexible knee
  - long lower leg bones
- shorter arms
- less-curved fingers

The Earliest Hominins

Data derived from molecular clock research suggests that the first hominins in the fossil record should be found in deposits that range from 5 million to 7 million years old, in East Africa. During that time, it is presumed that some form of apes began to develop hominin-like features. Regretfully, the fossil record of this stage of ape evolution is woefully lacking. For the few specimens that are available, it is difficult to ascertain without a doubt whether the species in question are true hominins, apes, or something in between. Having said that, the search for the earliest hominin continues, and several exciting recent discoveries continue to push the origins of ancestral humans farther back in time.

Sahelanthropus tchadensis (Late Miocene, 6 million to 7 million years ago, Chad). French anthropologist Michel Brunet led an expedition to the deserts of Chad, in north central Africa, in 2001 and 2002. Although located far from the usual stomping ground for hominin remains, these desert deposits offered up what now has been recognized by some scientists as the oldest known hominin species, *Sahelanthropus tchadensis* ("the Sahara hominin from Chad"). The specimen was nicknamed "Toumai" after the Chadian phrase for "hope of life." Consisting of a nearly complete cranium, a mandible (lower jaw), and several isolated teeth, the specimen was dated to about 7 million years ago. Reconstruction of the skull suggests that the foramen magnum was positioned far enough beneath the skull to accommodate a bipedal posture.

Lacking much more than these pieces, however, many paleontologists at first were reluctant to accept *Sahelanthropus* as the oldest hominin. They thought that the specimen probably was an ape showing some transitional features of the skull and jaw. Milford H. Wolpoff, for one, believed that some of the supposed features of the skull, such as the position of the foramen magnum, are disputable because of the incompleteness of the material. Wolpoff also argued that the anatomy of the face and jaws clearly show that *Sahelanthropus* did not normally hold its head aloft.

Wolpoff and several colleagues concluded that "*Sahelanthropus* was an ape living in an environment that was later inhabited by australopithecines and, like them, it adapted with a powerful masticatory complex."

In 2005, however, the French team discovered additional teeth and jaw fragments of the same age. These show that *Sahelanthropus* indeed lacked the large canines associated with the shearing bite of apes and had molars that showed hominin-like enamel. These finds strengthened the case for *Sahelanthropus* as the earliest hominin, although this matter is still disputed among scientists. *Sahelanthropus* is not entirely hominin-like, however; it includes such ape features as a U-shaped tooth battery, small brain size, and a somewhat flat face.

The presence of *Sahelanthropus* well outside the Great Rift Valley by the late Miocene is also notable to those interested in the radiation of hominins to Asia. The earliest hominins known from Asia at present are from the genera *Homo*. Could it be that some remains of hominins ancestral to *Homo* may also be found in Asia one day?

Orrorin tugenensis (Late Miocene, 6 million years ago, Kenya). Discovered in Kenya and described by paleoanthropologists Martin Pickford of Kenya and Brigitte Senut of the Laboratoire de Paleontologie du Museum National d'Histoire Naturelle, in Paris, *Orrorin tugenensis* is known from dental and postcranial skeletal elements. These were found in deposits that date from 6 million years ago. The fragmentary remains make it difficult to ascertain with certainty whether *Orrorin tugenensis* was a hominin or an ape. Among the most diagnostic material are parts of a thigh bone, but this material is not enough by itself to indicate bipedality with certainty. Senut describes the speciment as being a cross between ape and hominin. She explains, "The front teeth are closer to those of apes . . . but the back teeth are clearly more human in their square shape, their gracility and their enamel thickness." The apelike size of the canine argues against *Orrorin tugenensis* being a hominin.

Ardipithecus ramidus and *Ardipithecus kadabba* (Early Pliocene to Late Miocene, 4.4 million to 5.8 million years ago, Ethiopia). A fossil site along the Awash River in northern Ethiopia has yielded fragmentary remains of several individual hominin-like creatures. Initial work in 1992 by an international team of researchers garnered many jaw fragments, teeth, limb bones, and some cranial elements. These specimens originally were thought to be fossils of *Australopithecus* (see below). The team later revised its thinking on closer consideration of the limbs, teeth, and other features that appeared to be more primitive than those of australopithicines. Consequently, the name *Ardithiphecus ramidus* ("ground living root hominin") was given to the specimen.

Additional specimens were announced in 2004, and these were even older: They dated from as long ago as 5.8 million years. These specimens were even more apelike, and the team decided to designate them as a separate species, *Ardithiphecus kadabba*. It was also of interest that the habitat in which *Ardithiphecus* once lived was not the open, grassy plain normally associated with ancestral humans, but a dense forest in which other early primate fossils have been found. This suggests that *Ardithiphecus* was a hominin with forest-dwelling habits similar to those of modern gorillas.

Hominins of the Pliocene

The genus *Australopithecus* is perhaps the best candidate for a direct ancestor of *Homo*. *Australopithecus* existed for much of the Pliocene Epoch, and the apparent extinction of the genus coincides closely with the appearance of the first *Homo* species. Australopithecines were clearly bipedal. Their molars have the distinctively thick enamel characteristic of hominins, and there are measurable increases in the size of their brains during the 2 million years of their existence. They are found in the eastern and southern regions of Africa, where the remains of different species appear to have arisen at about the same time. Australopithecines were short compared with modern humans.

Australopithecus afarensis gathering fruit

Some of the later australopithecines are sometimes described as being either robust or gracile. Robust species were heavily built, with heavy muscles and thick bones. Their skulls were tall, with a thick lower jaw and massive molar teeth. The face of a robust hominin was flat, with thick cheekbones. The top of the skull had a small, bony crest down its midline that served as an additional place to attach the heavy muscles needed to increase the chewing force of its massive jaws.

Gracile australopithecines had a more slender bone structure and exhibited a general reduction in many of the same features associated with robust hominins. The molars were still large, but the jaws and associated muscles were not quite as massive. The face was not so flat and developed a short snout. The crest on top of the smaller skull cap was greatly reduced or lost.

Despite their primitive characteristics, the robust australopithecines were among some of the later species known from this genus. The lineage of most of these ancestral human species did not evidently lead to the development of increasingly well-adapted successors, but to the dead end called extinction.

Australopithecus anamensis (early Pliocene, 3.9 million to 4.2 million years ago, Kenya). A team led by Meave Leakey discovered the earliest known species of *Australopithecus* in 1995. Dating from about 4.2 million years ago, *Australopithecus anamensis* ("southern ape of the lake") was found in the Lake Turkana region of Kenya, an environment that comprised a savannahlike habitat in the early Pliocene. If the team had discovered only the jaws, which retained fairly large canines and some shearing action, this species might have been thought to be a species of ape. Remains of the limb bones, however, clearly show that *Australopithecus anamensis* walked on two legs. There is variation in the size of individuals, suggesting that males may have been larger than females. The mandible and dental battery of *A. anamensis* are primitive enough to distinguish this species from later australopithicines, particularly *A. afarensis*.

Australopithecus afarensis (middle Pliocene, 2.9 million to 3.9 million years ago, Ethiopia). *Australopithecus afarensis* is known from more than 70 specimens. It is the best-understood species of ancestral human. Discovered and first described by American paleontologist Donald Johanson (b. 1943) in 1974, the first specimen was that of a small female individual that measured only 3.5 feet (1 m) tall. Nicknamed Lucy, after the Beatles' song "Lucy in the Sky with Diamonds," *A. afarensis* was remarkably well preserved for a hominin specimen. Twenty percent of the skeleton was found, including bits of skull, jaws, teeth, ribs, pelvis, spine, arms, and legs. *A. afarensis* was unquestionably bipedal yet primitive in many other aspects of its anatomy. Lucy's brain was about as big as that of a modern chimpanzee. The arms of *A. afarensis* are longer than in

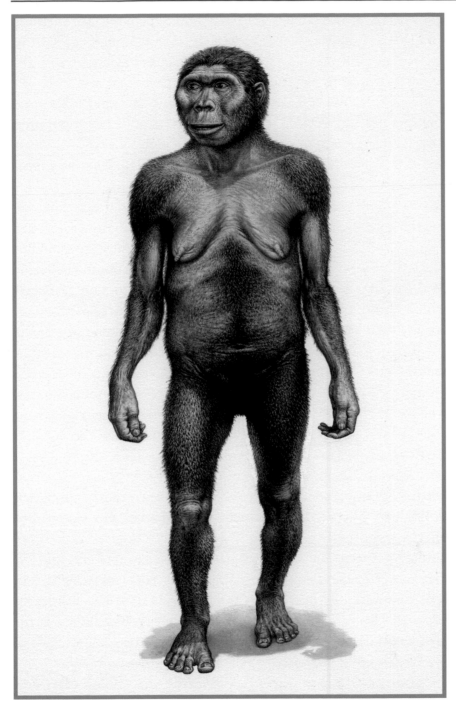

Australopithecus afarensis: Life restoration of the Lucy specimen

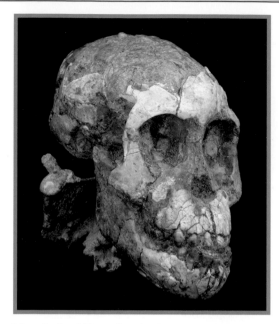

The skull of "Lucy"—she is known from more than 70 specimens, making it the best-understood species of ancestral human.

later hominins, and this ancestral human may have had curved fingers, a feature associated with the arboreal lifestyle of apes. The jaw of Lucy did not show the parabolic curvature of later hominins. Instead, it had a U-shape, with parallel rows of teeth, that was more akin to apes.

A set of fossilized footprints discovered in Tanzania and associated with *A. afarensis* provides a unique look at ancestral hominin behavior. Dating from 3.6 million years ago, the **trackway** includes prints made by two individuals, one larger than the other, walking side by side. The trackway stretches for 75 feet (23 m). The footprints reveal arched soles and a strolling gait consisting of slow, short strides.

Kenyanthropus platyops (middle Pliocene, 3.5 million years ago, Kenya): A somewhat contentious specimen is that of *Kenyanthropus platyops*, described in 2001 by Meave Leakey and her colleagues. There is disagreement as to whether this is a unique species or another example of *A. afarensis*. In support of her case, Leakey points to the smaller molars (a primitive feature) and the flat face of *Kenyanthropus* to distinguish it from *Australopithecus*. The implication is startling in that it means that several lineages of extinct hominins were living side by side in East Africa at the time. This implication adds complexity to the discussion of evolutionary linkages to *Homo*.

Australopithecus garhi (late Pliocene, 2.5 million years ago, Ethiopia): *A. garhi* was found in Ethiopia and is known from cranial and limb remains. It lived at a slightly more recent time than

A. afarensis and is distinguished by having larger molars and premolars and somewhat larger canine teeth. Another unusual and more derived feature are its longer arms and legs, which are more like those of *Homo*. Equally significantly, the remains of *A. garhi* were found along with animal bones that showed signs of having been butchered with tools: early evidence for toolmaking among hominins.

Australopithecus africanus (late Pliocene, 2.0 million to 3.5 million years ago, South Africa). This australopithecine species hails from southern Africa and includes the famous "Taung child" described earlier. *A. africanus* is more derived than other australopithecines in several ways. It has a slightly larger braincase, smaller front teeth, a rounded skull cap, and a less protruding face. It was a small hominin and traditionally has been grouped with the gracile australopithecines. It probably weighed between 70 and 100 pounds (32 to 45 kg).

Paranthropus aethiopicus and Paranthropus boisei (late Pliocene, 1.2 million to 2.7 million years ago, Kenya) and *Paranthropus robustus* (late Pliocene, 1.5 million to 2.0 million years ago, South Africa). Among the robust australopithecines were these species that lived in East Africa and South Africa. There has been a long-standing dispute over the proper naming of *Paranthropus*; some researchers consider it a species of *Australopithecus*. Of the two East African species, *P. boisei* was much smaller than *P. aethiopicus*. *P. boisei* had an estimated body weight of only 40 pounds (18 kg), which is smaller than a chimpanzee. *P. aethiopicus* was nearly twice that weight. In southern Africa, *A. robustus* was smaller still, with a weight of about 36 pounds (16 kg). The molars of *P. boisei* were more massive than those of any earlier hominin and had begun to take on a parabolic shape for the dental battery as in later hominins.

Each of these three *Paranthropus* species exhibited the cranial features associated with the robust descriptor: a bony crest on the midline of the skull (possibly only in males), a broad face, massive teeth, and a deep lower jaw. The dentition is so specialized that it

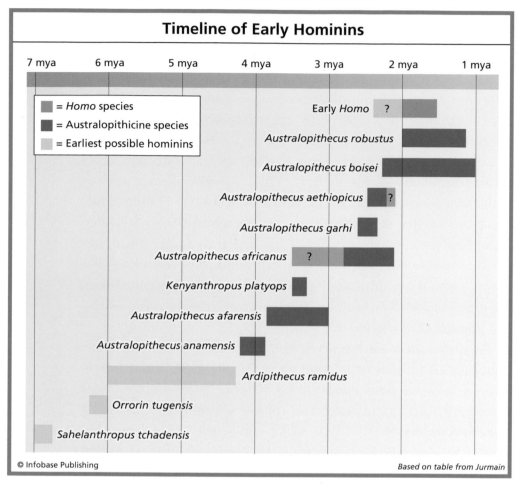

Timeline of Early Hominins

| 7 mya | 6 mya | 5 mya | 4 mya | 3 mya | 2 mya | 1 mya |

- = *Homo* species
- = Australopithicine species
- = Earliest possible hominins

Early *Homo* ?

Australopithecus robustus

Australopithecus boisei

Australopithecus aethiopicus ?

Australopithecus garhi

Australopithecus africanus ?

Kenyanthropus platyops

Australopithecus afarensis

Australopithecus anamensis

Ardipithecus ramidus

Orrorin tugensis

Sahelanthropus tchadensis

© Infobase Publishing   *Based on table from Jurmain*

Timeline of Early Hominins

appears that such robust species may have been highly adapted for a particular kind of tough vegetation or roots. The massive teeth and the jaw musculature are more derived—more highly adapted—than those of early *Homo*, indicating that robust australopithecines had veered away from the evolutionary lineage that may have led to the rise of *Homo*.

The accompanying diagram shows the positions in time of the ancestral human species discussed in this chapter.

SUMMARY

This chapter explored the rise of early hominins and described the most significant known species prior to the appearance of the genus *Homo*.

1. Fossil clues to the existence of possible early hominins can be found in rocks that date from between 5 million and 7 million years ago, in the late Miocene Epoch.
2. Africa is the cradle of early hominin evolution.
3. East Africa has produced many extraordinary hominin specimens from a geologically rugged area known as the Great Rift Valley.
4. Specimens of possible hominins that are older than 5 million years include *Sahelanthropus, Orrorin, and Ardithiphecus.*
5. The genus *Australopithecus* is the best candidate for a direct ancestor of *Homo*.
6. Some of the later, most derived australopithecines often are described as either robust or gracile. Robust species were more heavily built and had powerful jaws and teeth. Their skulls were tall, with a thick lower jaw and massive molar teeth. Gracile australopithecines had a more slender bone structure and exhibited a general reduction in many of the same features associated with robust hominins.
7. *Australopithecus afarensis* is known from more than 70 specimens. This makes it the best-understood species of ancestral human. The best-known and most complete specimen is nicknamed Lucy and represents a small female individual.
8. Several different lineages of ancestral humans appear to have lived at the same time, in Africa, during the middle Pliocene Epoch.
9. The massive teeth and jaw musculature of *Paranthropus* are more derived—more highly adapted—than those of early *Homo*, indicating that robust australopithecines had veered away from the evolutionary lineage that may have led to the rise of *Homo*.

CONCLUSION

The wealth of fossils of ancestral humans from the late Miocene and Pliocene forms a complicated puzzle—a maze of evolutionary links and dead ends in the lineage of the hominins. Through the relentless dedication of field researchers in recent decades, the picture of hominin evolution is becoming increasingly clear. The hub of ape evolution was eastern Africa, along the area where the Great Rift Valley was developing. The earliest fossils of true apes are known from Kenya, Namibia, Uganda, and Ethiopia. As the lineages of apes diminished by the end of the Miocene, the apes also diverged onto two evolutionary paths. One path split off between 13 million and 15 million years ago and led to orangutans. The other path led to modern African apes and, eventually, to humans. Humans split from the lineage of *Pan* (the chimpanzee) between 5 million and 7 million years ago.

Fossil evidence for early hominins from the late Miocene is scant and often controversial. It is clear, however, that by about 4.2 million years ago, in the Pliocene, ancestral humans were well established on the savannahs of Africa. The hominin adaptations of bipedalism and an increasingly generalized dental battery well suited for a varied diet gave early hominins an adaptive advantage. Before very long, hominins of the Pliocene Epoch had left the forests of their ape ancestors and broadened their range of influence across the open grasslands that stretched through Africa. Soon, hominins migrated northward out of Africa to occupy Europe, Asia, and other parts of the globe as anatomically modern humans of the genus *Homo*. The story of *Homo* evolution is the subject of another book in *The Prehistoric Earth*: *Early Humans*.

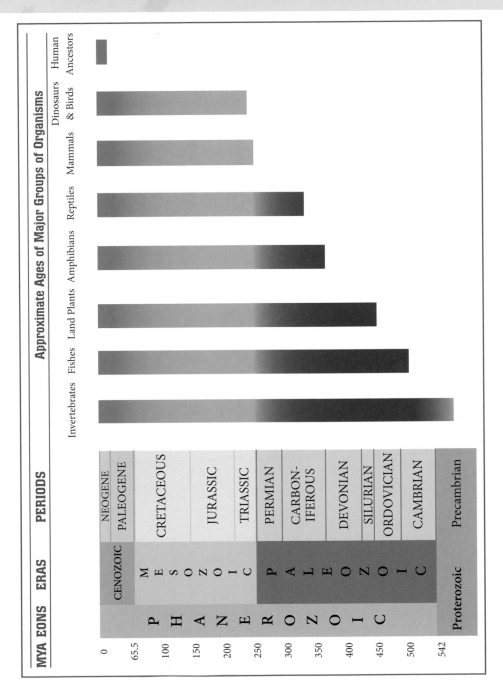

APPENDIX TWO: POSITIONAL TERMS

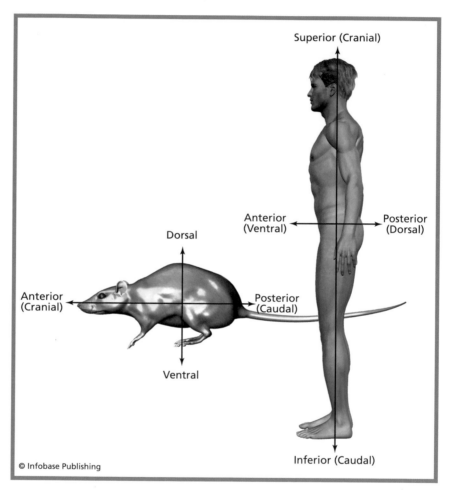

Positional terms used to describe vertebrate anatomy

GLOSSARY

adaptations   Anatomical, physiological, and behavioral changes that occur in an organism that enable it to survive environmental changes.

anatomy   The basic biological systems of an animal, such as the skeletal and muscular systems.

anterior   Directional term meaning toward the head, or cranial, end of a vertebrate.

anthropoids   Higher primates (monkeys, apes, and humans).

anthropologist   Scientist who studies the biological and cultural evolution of humans.

anthropology   The study of biological and cultural human evolution.

australopithecines   Genera of ancestral humans who date primarily from the Pliocene Epoch.

basal   At or near the base or earliest level of evolutionary development; a term usually used to refer to an ancestral taxon.

binocular vision   Overlapping vision of the two eyes.

bipedalism   Walking upright on two legs.

brachiation   Swinging from branch to branch using grasping arms and legs.

carnivorous   Meat-eating.

clade   A group of related organisms including all the descendants of a single common ancestor.

culture   The accumulation of acquired and learned behaviors shared by a population of organisms.

derived   Term used to describe a trait of an organism that is a departure from the most basal (ancestral) form.

diurnal   Active during the day.

DNA   Deoxyribonucleic acid, the molecule that carries genetic code and that is found in every living cell of an organism. Genes are located on strands of DNA.

encephalization quotient   (EQ) Also known as a brain-to-body-mass ratio; a ratio that compares the actual brain mass of an animal with the expected brain mass of an animal of that size.

eutherian   Mammal that gives birth to live young after an extended gestation period during which the embryo is nourished by means of a placenta, a temporary organ found in females during pregnancy; also called a "placental" mammal.

evolution   The natural process by which species gradually change over time, controlled by changes to the genetic code—the DNA—of organisms and whether or not those changes enable an organism to survive in a given environment.

extant   Term used to describe an organism that is living today; not extinct.

extinction   The irreversible elimination of an entire species of organism because it cannot adapt effectively to changes in its environment.

femur   Upper leg bone.

foramen magnum   A hole in the bony base of the skull that marks the point of connection between the skull and the vertebral column.

forelimbs   The two front legs of a vertebrate.

fossil   Any physical trace or remains of prehistoric life.

gene   A portion of a DNA strand that controls a particular inherited trait.

gene flow   The introduction of new alleles from an outside population of the same species.

gene pool   The combined genetic makeup of a species population.

genetic drift   A chance fluctuation in allele frequency in a gene pool that is not caused by natural selection.

genome   The complete genetic instructions embodied in the DNA of a species.

genus   (plural: genera) A taxonomic name entity for one or more closely related organisms that is divided into species; names of organisms, such as *Tyrannosaurus rex*, are composed of two parts: the genus name (first) and the species name (second).

geographic isolation   The isolation of species on a land formation as a result of naturally occurring geologic events (e.g., formation of an island or of mountains).

gradualism   The emergence of new species as a slow and gradual process.

herbivore   An animal whose primary food source is vegetation.

heterodont   Having different kinds of teeth in different zones of the jaw.

hind limbs   The two rear legs of a vertebrate.

hominin   (alternatively: hominid) Fossil and living humans.

Homo sapiens   Modern human species.

macroevolution   The evolutionary process that results in new species.

metabolism   The combination of all biochemical processes that take place in an organism to keep it alive.

microevolution   The genetic changes that can take place within a species population.

molecular clock   A mathematical model for estimating when two species diverged in the distant past by comparing genetic differences between species and establishing a time scale required for such changes to accumulate.

morphological   Pertaining to the body form and structure of an organism.

mutation   Any change in the genetic code; mutations occur at random.

natural selection   One of Darwin's observations regarding the way in which evolution works; given the complex and changing conditions under which life exists, those individuals with the combination of inherited traits best suited to a particular environment will survive and reproduce while others will not.

neural   Pertaining to the nerves or nervous system; term used to describe nerves and associated connections to the brain.

New World   The Americas.

nocturnal   Active during the night.

Old World   Africa, Asia, and Europe.

omnivorous   Eating a diet consisting of both plants and meat.

opposable   Word used to describe a thumb or big toe that can flex against—that is, in opposition to—the other digits, making it possible to grasp objects: a trait of primates.

paleoanthropologist   Scientist who studies human origins using fossils as a key source of information.

paleoanthropology   Study of biological aspects of human origins and evolution; the study of primate and hominin fossils.

paleontologist   Scientist who studies prehistoric life, usually using fossils.

phylogeny   The family tree of a group of related organisms based on shared, inherited traits.

population   Members of the same species that live in a particular area.

population genetics   The study of the frequency of alleles, genotypes, and phenotypes in a given group of individuals.

postcranial   "Behind the head"; term generally used to refer to the portion of the vertebrate skeleton other than the head.

posterior   Directional term meaning toward the tail end; also known as the caudal end.

predator   Animal that actively seeks, kills, and feeds on other animals.

primatology   The study of living primates.

prosimians   Lower primates (lemurs, lorises, and tarsiers).

punctuated equilibria   Rapid evolutionary changes caused when a population of a given species suddenly encounters a dramatic change to its habitat.

sedimentary   Word used to describe layers of rock deposited over time; sedimentary rock may contain fossils.

sexual dimorphism   Variation in morphology between males and females of a species.

speciation   The evolution of new species.

species   In classification, the most basic biological unit of living organisms; members of a species can interbreed and produce fertile offspring.

taxa   (singular: taxon) In classification, a taxon is a group of related organisms, such as a clade, genus, or species.

taxonomy   The discipline of classifying organisms.

theory   A comprehensive, testable explanation about some aspect of the natural world that is backed by an extensive body of facts over time.

theory of acquired characteristics   An early theory of evolution, now proved to be incorrect, stating that an organism could be altered by circumstantial changes in the environment and that such alterations could be passed along to offspring.

tibia   Lower leg bone.

trackway   Series of sequential animal footprints.

transitional   Representing one step in the many stages that exist as a species evolves.

CHAPTER BIBLIOGRAPHY

Preface

Wilford, John Noble. "When No One Read, Who Started to Write?" *New York Times* (April, 6, 1999). Available online. URL: *http://query.nytimes.com/gst/fullpage.html?res=9B01EFD61139F935A35757C0A96F958260*. Accessed March 31, 2008.

Chapter 1 – The History of Evolutionary Thought

Haviland, William A., Harald E.L. Prins, Dana Walrath, and Bunny McBride. *Anthropology: The Human Challenge*, 12th ed. New York: Wadsworth, 2008.

Jurmain, Robert, Lynn Kilgore, and Wenda Trevathan. *Introduction to Physical Anthropology*, 10th ed. New York: Wadsworth, 2005.

Kottak, Conrad Phillip. *Anthropology: The Exploration of Human Diversity*, 12th ed. New York: McGraw-Hill, 2008.

Park, Michael Alan. *Biological Anthropology*, 5th ed. New York: McGraw-Hill, 2008.

———, ed. *Biological Anthropology: An Introductory Reader*, 5th ed. New York: McGraw-Hill, 2008.

Chapter 2 – Mechanisms of Evolution

Casey, Denise, Charles Cantor, and Sylvia Spengler. *Primer on Molecular Genetics*. Human Genome Management Information System. Oak Ridge National Laboratory, U.S. Department of Energy, 1992.

Chimpanzee Sequencing and Analysis Consortium. "Initial Sequence of the Chimpanzee Genome and Comparison with the Human Genome." *Nature* 437 (September 1, 2005): 69–87.

Haviland, William A., Harald E.L. Prins, Dana Walrath, and Bunny McBride. *Anthropology: The Human Challenge*, 12th ed. New York: Wadsworth, 2008.

Jurmain, Robert, Lynn Kilgore, and Wenda Trevathan. *Introduction to Physical Anthropology*, 10th ed. New York: Wadsworth, 2005.

Kottak, Conrad Phillip. *Anthropology: The Exploration of Human Diversity*, 12th ed. New York: McGraw-Hill, 2008.

Park, Michael Alan. *Biological Anthropology*, 5th ed. New York: McGraw-Hill, 2008.

———, ed. *Biological Anthropology: An Introductory Reader*, 5th ed. New York: McGraw-Hill, 2008.

Stein, Philip L., and Bruce M. Rowe. *Physical Anthropology*, 8th ed. New York: McGraw-Hill, 2003.

Turner, Alan, and Mauricio Anton. *Evolving Eden*. New York: Columbia University Press, 2004.

Wallace, D.R. *Beasts of Eden*. Berkeley: University of California Press, 2004.

Chapter 3 – Origin and Classification of the Primates

Benton, Michael. *Vertebrate Paleontology*, 3rd ed. Oxford: Blackwell Publishing, 2005.

Carroll, Sean B. "Genetics and the Making of *Homo sapiens*." *Nature* 422 (April 24, 2003): 849–857.

Ember, Carol R., Melvin Ember, and Peter N. Peregrine. *Anthropology*, 11th ed. Upper Saddle River, N.J.: Prentice Hall, 2005.

Jurmain, Robert, Lynn Kilgore, and Wenda Trevathan. *Introduction to Physical Anthropology*, 10th ed. New York: Wadsworth, 2005.

Kemp, T.S. *The Origin and Evolution of Mammals*. Oxford: Oxford University Press, 2005.

Kottak, Conrad Phillip. *Anthropology: The Exploration of Human Diversity*, 12th ed. New York: McGraw-Hill, 2008.

Park, Michael Alan, ed. *Biological Anthropology: An Introductory Reader*, 5th ed. New York: McGraw-Hill, 2008.

Stanford, Craig, John S. Allen, and Susan C. Antón. *Biological Anthropology*. Upper Saddle River, N.J.: Prentice Hall, 2006.

Wolpoff, Milford H. *Paleoanthropology*, 2nd ed. New York: McGraw-Hill, 1999.

Chapter 4 – Primate Biology and Behavior

"Evolution of the Brain." *Nature* 447, no. 7146 (June 14, 2007): 753.

Dennis, Carina. "Branching Out." *Nature* 437 (September 1, 2005): 18–19.

Di Fiore, Anthony. "Molecular Genetic Approaches to the Study of Primate Behavior, Social Organization, and Reproduction." *Yearbook of Physical Anthropology*. New York: Wiley, 2003: 63–99.

Ekman, Paul. "Facial Expressions," in Dalgleish, Tim, and Mick Power, eds. *Handbook of Cognition and Emotion.* New York: John Wiley & Sons, 1999.

Ember, Carol R., Melvin Ember, and Peter N. Peregrine. *Anthropology,* 11th ed. Upper Saddle River, N.J.: Prentice Hall, 2005.

Harrison, Terry. "Fossil Apes," *McGraw-Hill Encyclopedia of Science and Technology* 7 (2002): 456–459.

Jurmain, Robert, Lynn Kilgore, and Wenda Trevathan. *Introduction to Physical Anthropology,* 10th ed. New York: Wadsworth, 2005.

Kottak, Conrad Phillip. *Anthropology: The Exploration of Human Diversity,* 12th ed. New York: McGraw-Hill, 2008.

Mercader, Julio, Melissa Panger, and Christophe Boesch. "Excavation of a Chimpanzee Stone Tool Site in the African Rainforest." *Science* 296, no. 5572 (May 24, 2002): 1452–1455.

Patterson, Nick, Daniel J. Richter, Sante Gnerre, Eric S. Lander, and David Reich. "Genetic Evidence for Complex Speciation of Humans and Chimpanzees." *Nature* 441 (June 29, 2006): 1103–1108.

Stanford, Craig, John S. Allen, and Susan C. Antón. *Biological Anthropology.* Upper Saddle River, N.J.: Prentice Hall, 2006.

Trivedi, Bijal P. " 'Hot Tub Monkeys' Offer Eye on Nonhuman 'Culture.' " *National Geographic Channel,* February 6, 2004. Available online. URL: *http://news.nationalgeographic.com/news/2004/02/0206_040206_tvmacaques.html.* Accessed April 30, 2008.

Wolpoff, Milford H. *Paleoanthropology,* 2nd ed. New York: McGraw-Hill, 1999.

Chapter 5 – The Ape-Hominin Transition

"Evolution of the Brain." *Nature* 447, no. 7146 (June 14, 2007): 753.

"Great Ape Genomes Offer Insight into Human Evolution." *Public Library of Science.* July 13, 2004. Available online. URL: *http://www.pubmedcentral.nih.gov/articlerender.fcgi?artid=449907.* Accessed April 30, 2008.

Benton, Michael. *Vertebrate Paleontology,* 3rd ed. Oxford: Blackwell Publishing, 2005.

Dalton, Rex. "Oldest Gorilla Ages our Joint Ancestor." *Nature* 448 (August 23, 2007): 844–845.

Dennell, Robin, and Wil Roebroeks. "An Asian Perspective on Early Human Dispersal from Africa." *Nature* 438 (December 22/29, 2005): 1099–1104.

Ember, Carol R., Melvin Ember, and Peter N. Peregrine. *Anthropology*, 11th ed. Upper Saddle River, N.J.: Prentice Hall, 2005.

Fortna, Andrew, Young Kim, Erik MacLaren, Kriste Marshall, Gretchen Hahn, Lynne Meltesen, Matthew Brenton, Raquel Hink, Sonya Burgers, Tina Hernandez-Boussard, Anis Karimpour-Fard, Deborah Glueck, Loris McGavran, Rebecca Berry, Jonathan Pollack, and James M. Sikela. "Lineage-Specific Gene Duplication and Loss in Human and Great Ape Evolution." *Public Library of Science* 2, no. 7 (July 2004): 0937–0954.

Fuentes, Agustin. *Core Concepts in Biological Anthropology*. New York: McGraw-Hill, 2007.

Harrison, Terry, "Fossil Apes," *McGraw-Hill Encyclopedia of Science and Technology* 7 (2002): 456–459.

Johanson, Donald, and Maitland Edey. *Lucy: The Beginnings of Humankind*. New York: Simon and Schuster, 1981.

Kottak, Conrad Phillip. *Anthropology: The Exploration of Human Diversity*, 12th ed. New York: McGraw-Hill, 2008.

Kunimatsu, Yutaka, Masato Nakatsukasa, Yoshihiro Sawada, Tetsuya Sakai, Masayuki Hyodo, Hironobu Hyodo, Tetsumaru Itaya, Hideo Nakaya, Haruo Saegusa, Arnaud Mazurier, Mototaka Saneyoshi, Hiroshi Tsujikawa, Ayumi Yamamoto, and Emma Mbua. "A New Late Miocene Great Ape from Kenya and its Implications for the Origins of African Great Apes and Humans." *Proceedings of the National Academy of Sciences of the United States*, 104 (2007): 19220–19225.

Latimer, B.M., and C.O. Lovejoy. "Hallucal Tarsometatarsal Joint in *Australopithecus afarensis.*" *American Journal of Physical Anthropology* 82, no. 2 (1990): 125–133.

Miller, Barbara D., and Bernard Wood. *Anthropology*. New York: Allyn and Bacon, 2006.

Stanford, Craig, John S. Allen, and Susan C. Antón. *Biological Anthropology*. Upper Saddle River, N.J.: Prentice Hall, 2006.

Stein, Philip L., and Bruce M. Rowe. *Physical Anthropology*, 8th ed. New York: McGraw-Hill, 2003.

Takahata, Naoyuki, and Yoko Satta. "Evolution of the Primate Lineage Leading to Modern Humans: Phylogenetic and Demographic Inferences from DNA Sequences." *Proceedings of the National Academy of Science of the United States* 94 (April 1997): 4811–4815.

Templeton, Alan R. "Out of Africa Again and Again." *Nature* 416 (March 7, 2002): 45–51.

Wakely, John. "Complex speciation of humans and chimpanzees." *Nature* 452 (March 13, 2008): E3–E4

Wilson, A.C., and V.M. Sarich. "A Molecular Time Scale for Human Evolution." *Proceedings of the National Academy of Sciences of the United States* 69 (1969): 1088–1093.

Wolpoff, Milford H., Brigitte Senut, Martin Pickford, and John Hawks. "*Sahelanthropus* or *Sahelpithecus*?" *Nature* 419 (October 10, 2002): 581–582.

Wood, Bernard. "A Precious Little Bundle." *Nature* 443 (September 21, 2006): 279–280.

Zollikofer, Christoph P.E., Marcia S. Ponce de León, Daniel E. Lieberman, Franck Guy, David Pilbeam, Andossa Likius, Hassane T. Mackaye, Patrick Vignaud, and Michel Brunet. "Virtual Cranial Reconstruction of *Sahelanthropus tchadensis*." *Nature* 434 (April 7, 2005): 755.

Chapter 6 – The Earliest Human Ancestors

Alemseged, Zeresenay, Fred Spoor, William H. Kimbel, René Bobe, Denis Geraads, Denne Reed, and Jonathan G. Wynn. "A Juvenile Early Hominin Skeleton from Dikika, Ethiopia." *Nature* 443 (September 21, 2006): 296–301.

Alexander, Richard D. "How Did Humans Evolve?" Museum of Zoology, University of Michigan. *Special Publication No. 1* (1990): 1–38.

Benton, Michael. *Vertebrate Paleontology*, 3rd ed. Oxford: Blackwell Publishing, 2005.

Brunet, Michel, Franck Guy, David Pilbeam, Daniel E. Lieberman, Andossa Likius, Hassane T. Mackaye, Marcia S. Ponce de León, Christoph P.E. Zollikofer, and Patrick Vignaud. "New Material of the Earliest Hominid from the Upper Miocene of Chad." *Nature* 434 (April 7, 2005): 752–755.

Carbonell, Eudald, José M. Bermúdez de Castro, Josep M. Parés, Alfredo Pérez-González, Gloria Cuenca-Bescós, Andreu Olle, Marina Mosquera, Rosa Huguet, Jan van der Made, Antonio Rosas, Robert Sala, Josep Vallverdú, Nuria García, Darryl E. Granger, María Martinón-Torres, Xosé P. Rodríguez, Greg M. Stock, Josep M. Vergés, Ethel Allué, Francesc Burjachs, Isabel Cáceres, Antoni Canals, Alfonso Benito, Carlos Díez, Marina Lozano, Ana Mateos, Marta Navazo, Jesús Rodríguez, Jordi Rosell, and Juan L. Arsuaga. "The First Hominin of Europe." *Nature* 452, no. 7146 (March 27, 2008): 465–470.

Carroll, Sean B. "Genetics and the Making of *Homo sapiens*." *Nature* 422 (April 24, 2003): 849–857.

Ember, Carol R., Melvin Ember, and Peter N. Peregrine. *Anthropology*, 11th ed. Upper Saddle River, N.J.: Prentice Hall, 2005.

Fuentes, Agustin. *Core Concepts in Biological Anthropology*. New York: McGraw-Hill, 2007.

Kottak, Conrad Phillip. *Anthropology: The Exploration of Human Diversity*, 12th ed. New York: McGraw-Hill, 2008.

Lordkipanidze, David, Tea Jashashvili, Abesalom Vekua, Marcia S. Ponce de León, Christoph P.E. Zollikofer, G. Philip Rightmire, Herman Pontzer, Reid Ferring, Oriol Oms, Martha Tappen, Maia Bukhsianidze, Jordi Agusti, Ralf Kahlke, Gocha Kiladze, Bienvenido Martinez-Navarro, Alexander Mouskhelishvili, Medea Nioradze, and Lorenzo Rook. "Postcranial Evidence from Early Homo from Dmanisi, Georgia." *Nature* 449, no. 7146 (September 20, 2007): 306–310.

Miller, Barbara D., and Bernard Wood. *Anthropology*. New York: Allyn and Bacon, 2006.

Senut, Brigitte. "First Hominid from the Miocene (Lukeino Formation, Kenya)." *Earth and Planetary Sciences* 332 (2001): 137–144.

Spoor, F., M.G. Leakey, P.N. Gathogo, F.H. Brown, S.C. Antón, I. McDougall, C. Kiarie, F.K. Manthi, and L.N. Leakey. "Implications of New Early *Homo* Fossils from Ileret, East of Lake Turkana, Kenya." *Nature* 448 (August 9, 2007): 689–691.

Stanford, Craig, John S. Allen, and Susan C. Antón. *Biological Anthropology*. Upper Saddle River, N.J.: Prentice Hall, 2006.

Stein, Philip L. "Hominin or Hominid? What's in a Name!" Available online. URL: *http://www.anthro.utah.edu/PDFs/courses/broughton/stein.pdf*. Accessed May 1, 2008.

Stein, Philip L., and Bruce M. Rowe. *Physical Anthropology*, 8th ed. New York: McGraw-Hill, 2003.

Templeton, Alan R. "Out of Africa Again and Again." *Nature* 416 (March 7, 2002): 45–51.

FURTHER READING

Benton, Michael. *Vertebrate Paleontology*, 3rd ed. Oxford: Blackwell Publishing, 2005.

Ellis, Richard. *No Turning Back: The Life and Death of Animal Species*. New York: HarperCollins, 2004.

Ember, Carol R., Melvin Ember, and Peter N. Peregrine. *Anthropology*, 11th ed. Upper Saddle River, N.J.: Prentice Hall, 2005.

Fuentes, Agustin. *Core Concepts in Biological Anthropology*. New York: McGraw-Hill, 2007.

Haviland, William A., Harald E.L. Prins, Dana Walrath, and Bunny McBride. *Anthropology: The Human Challenge*, 12th ed. New York: Wadsworth, 2008.

Jurmain, Robert, Lynn Kilgore, and Wenda Trevathan. *Introduction to Physical Anthropology*, 10th ed. New York: Wadsworth, 2005.

Kemp, T.S. *The Origin and Evolution of Mammals*. Oxford: Oxford University Press, 2005.

Kottak, Conrad Phillip. *Anthropology: The Exploration of Human Diversity*, 12th ed. New York: McGraw-Hill, 2008.

Miller, Barbara D., and Bernard Wood. *Anthropology*. New York: Allyn and Bacon, 2006.

Park, Michael Alan. *Biological Anthropology*, 5th ed. New York: McGraw-Hill, 2008.

———, ed. *Biological Anthropology: An Introductory Reader*, 5th ed. New York: McGraw-Hill, 2008.

Prothero, Donald R. *After the Dinosaurs: The Age of Mammals*. Bloomington: Indiana University Press, 2006.

Raven, Peter H., George B. Johnson, Jonathan B. Losos, and Susan R. Singer. *Biology,* 7th ed. New York: McGraw-Hill, 2005.

Stanford, Craig, John S. Allen, and Susan C. Antón. *Biological Anthropology*. Upper Saddle River, N.J: Prentice Hall, 2006.

Stein, Philip L., and Bruce M. Rowe. *Physical Anthropology*, 8th ed. New York: McGraw-Hill, 2003.

Turner, Alan, and Mauricio Anton. *Evolving Eden*. New York: Columbia University Press, 2004.

Wallace, D.R. *Beasts of Eden*. Berkeley: University of California Press, 2004.

Wolpoff, Milford H. *Paleoanthropology*, 2nd ed. New York: McGraw-Hill, 1999.

Web Sites

BBC. Human Beginnings

A collection of text and video content related to the evolution of humans, sponsored by the British Broadcasting Corporation.

http://www.bbc.co.uk/sn/prehistoric_life/human/

International Commission on Stratigraphy. International Stratigraphic Chart

Downloadable geologic time scales provided by the International Commission on Stratigraphy.

http://www.stratigraphy.org/cheu.pdf

Maddison, D.R., and K.-S. Schulz. The Tree of Life Web Project

The Tree of Life Web Project is a meticulously designed view of life-forms based on their phylogenetic (evolutionary) connections. It is hosted by the University of Arizona College of Agriculture and Life Sciences and the University of Arizona Library.

http://tolweb.org/tree/phylogeny.html

National Museums of Kenya

Guide to museums in Kenya, many of which house important fossils of ancestral humans from East Africa.

http://www.museums.or.ke/

National Primate Research Center. University of Wisconsin, Primate Info Net

An excellent resource for scientific information about living primates. Includes fact sheets about different species and an audio-visual library of primate vocalizations and research video.

http://pin.primate.wisc.edu/index.html

Public Broadcasting Service. Evolution Library: Evidence for Evolution

This resource outlines the extensive evidence in support of both the fact and theory of evolution, basing its approach on studies of the fossil record, molecular sequences, and comparative anatomy.

http://www.pbs.org/wgbh/evolution/library/04/

Scotese, Christopher R. Paleomap Project

A valuable source of continental maps showing the positioning of Earth's continents over the course of geologic time.

http://www.scotese.com/

SOMSO Modelle, Reconstructions of Primate and Hominin Skulls

This is the Web site of a commercial maker of scientifically accurate skulls and skeletal bones of extinct apes and hominins. This link features a gallery of these images.

http://www.somso.de/index.htm?f=english/anatomie/stammesgeschichte.htm

Teaching About Evolution and the Nature of Science. Investigating Common Descent: Formulating Explanations and Models

This educational resource designed for high school science teachers provides background, research ideas, and facts regarding human evolution as defined by the National Research Council.

http://www.nap.edu/html/evolution98/evol6-d.html

University of California Museum of Paleontology. History of Evolutionary Thought

A tutorial about the thinkers who founded the modern science of evolutionary biology.

http://www.ucmp.berkeley.edu/history/evothought.html

University of Michigan Museum of Anthropology

The Museum of Anthropology is an internationally recognized center for anthropological and archaeological research. This Web site contains information about faculty research, the museum's organization, and selected images from its collections.

http://www.lsa.umich.edu/umma/

PICTURE CREDITS

Page

INDEX

A

Acquired characteristics, theory of, 29–30, 35–36
Adaptations, 48, 52–57, 61, 67–69
Affiliative behaviors, 95
Africa, 71–72, 80–81, 121–124, 135
Afropithecus, 77
Aggressive behaviors, 95
Alexander, Richard D., 113
Algeripithecus, 71
Alleles, 42–44, 60
Altitude, adaptation and, 53–56
American Sign Language, 89
Amino acids, 45
Anaximander, 19–20, 34
Andrews, Peter, 102
Animal Minds (Griffin), 112–113
Animals, chromosomes of, 54
Anthropoids, 64, 65. *See also* Haplorhines; New World monkeys; Old World monkeys
Anthropology, overview of, 13
Apes, 70–71, 83, 102–103, 107–108. *See also* Hominids; Hominoidea
Archonta, 64, 80

Ardipithecus kadabba, 128
Ardipithecus ramidus, 128
Ardithiphecus, 135
Aristotle, 20, 34
Australopithecines, 117
Australopithecus, 121–122, 128–133, 135
Australopithecus afarensis, 129–132, 135
Australopithecus africanus, 133
Australopithecus anamensis, 129
Austraopithecus garhi, 132–133
Awash River, 128

B

Baboons, 92, 93, 94–95
Beagle (HMS), 31
Beard, Christopher, 71–72
Bible, 22
Binocular vision, 87–88, 99
Biological adaptation, 52–57, 61
Bipedalism, 105–110, 117
"Bonded pair and offspring" social structure, 92
Bonobos, 93
Brachiation, 77
Brain stems, 114

Brains, 87–88, 99, 112–119
Brain-to-body-mass ratio, 115–118, 120
Brunet, Michael, 126–127

C

Capuchin monkeys, 97
Carnivora, 21
Catarrhines, 67–68, 80
Catopithecus, 72
Cerebellum, 114
Cerebral cortex, 114
Chance, evolution and, 50
Chimpanzee Sequencing and Analysis Consortium, 104
Chimpanzees, 76, 90–95, 97, 103–104
Chromosomes, 45–47, 54–55
Chuang Tsu, 20, 34
Classification, controversy over, 82–83
Color vision, 87
Communication, 95, 99, 112–113
Consciousness, 112–113
Corpus callosum, 114
Culture, 96–97, 98

D

Dart, Raymond, 122
Darwin, Charles evolution and, 26, 28, 30–34

Darwin, Charles
(*continued*)
  gradualism and, 57
  human species and, 82
  inheritance and,
    39–40
  on species, 15
  work of, 14
Darwin, Erasmus, 28
Diastomas, 110–111
Diets, 86, 91–92, 107,
  119
Diurnalism, 67
DNA, 19, 44–47, 54–55,
  60, 74–76
Dobzhansky,
  Theodosius, 52
Dominance hierarchies,
  94–95
Double helix, 45
Drift, genetic, 49
Dryopithecus, 78

E

Eldredge, Niles, 57
Emotions, 112–113
Encephalization
  quotients (EQ),
  115–118, 120
Endocasts, 113
Endocrine disruptors,
  114–115
Environment, evolution
  and, 32, 106–107
Enzymes, 45
Eosimias, 71–72, 81
EQ. *See* Encephalization
  quotients
Erect posture, 85–86
Erosion, 22–23
*Essay on the Principle of
  Population* (Malthus),
  30–31
Eutherian mammals, 64

Evolution
  biochemical basis of
    inheritance and,
    44–47
  biological adaptation
    and, 52–57
  brains and, 117–118
  chance, direction, and
    results of, 50–51
  Darwin and, 26, 28,
    30–33
  early understanding
    of, 19–20
  environment and, 32,
    106–107
  European geologists
    and, 21–26
  European taxonomists
    and, 20–21
  genetic, 47
  history of theory of,
    26–30
  individuals, popula-
    tions and, 47–50
  inheritance patterns
    and, 39–44
  macro, 50–52
  micro, 47–48, 60
  overview of, 14, 15,
    19, 35–37, 59–61
  principles of
    Darwinism and,
    33–35
  rate of, 57–59
Extinctions, 22, 51

F

Fayum Depression, 72
Feet, 84–85, 110
Femurs, 110
Finches, 31
Fission-fusion soci-
  eties, 93
Flowering plants, 58–59

Food resources, 91–92,
  107
Foramen magnum,
  107–108
Forelimbs, 84, 105

G

Galápagos Islands, 31
Gametes, 47
Garden of Eden, 22
Gardner, Beatrix and
  R. Allen, 89
Gene flow, 49
Gene pools, 47, 60
Genes, 42, 45, 104
Genetic adaptation, 53,
  54, 57, 61
Genetic drift, 49
Genetic evolution, 47
Genetics, 40–44, 104
Genomes, 44, 54–55, 61,
  104
Geographic isolation, 52,
  66–67
Geology, 21–25
Gibbons, 93
Gigantopithecus, 78
Giraffes, 29, 36
Goodall, Jane, 90
Gorillas, 90, 93, 103
Gould, Stephen Jay, 57
Gradualism, 35, 57, 61
Grasping hands and feet,
  84–85, 98
Great Ape Trust, 89–90
Great Flood, 22
Great Rift Valley, 80, 123,
  127
Griffin, Donald, 112–113

H

Hands, 84
Haplorhines, 65,
  67–78, 80

Hemoglobins, 74
Heterodont dentition, 86
Heterozygotes,
    42–44, 60
Hierarchies, 94–95
Hominids, overview of,
    102–103
Hominins
    anatomy of earliest,
        125
    bipedalism and,
        105–110
    brains and, 112–119
    defined, 103
    earliest, 121–124,
        126–128
    fossils of, 124–125
    human traits and,
        103–105
    overview of, 102–103,
        128–135
    of Pliocene, 128–135
    teeth, jaws and,
        110–112
Hominoidea, 67, 73,
    76–78
Homo species, 103,
    104–105, 120
Homozygotes,
    42–44, 60
Huffman, Michael, 96
Humans, evolution of,
    104–105
Humphrey, Nicholas K.,
    113
Hutton, James, 22–24,
    34, 37
Huxley, Thomas, 82–83
Hybrid differences, 52
Hypoxia, 53–57

I

Ibn Miskawayh, 20, 34
Imagination, 113

Imanishi, Kinji, 90
Incompatibility,
    physiological, 52
Individuals, genetic
    evolution and, 47–48
Inheritance. See also
    Evolution
    biochemical basis of,
        44–47
    discovery of patterns
        of, 39–44
    individuals, popula-
        tions and, 48–50
    phylogenies and,
        74–76
Intelligence, 88, 90,
    112–119
Isolation, 52, 66–67
Isotopes, 26
Itani, Junichiro, 90

J

Jaws, 67–69, 110–112
Jerison, Harry, 117
Johanson, Donald, 130

K

Kelley, Jay, 102
Kenyanthropus platyops,
    132
Kottak, Conrad, 13, 104,
    107

L

Lamarck, Jean-Baptiste,
    29–30, 34, 35–36, 37
Lamarckism, 29–30,
    30–36
Language, 95
Leakey, Louis and Mary,
    76, 124
Leakey, Meave, 124, 130,
    132
Leakey, Richard, 124

Learning, 96–97
Leclerc de Buffon,
    Georges-Louis, 34
Legs, 110
Lemurs, 66–67, 80, 83
Leonard, William, 119
Life cycles, 88
Limbs, 84–86
Linnaean Society, 32–33
Linnaeus, Carolus, 21,
    34, 37
Locomotion, 84–86, 98,
    105–110
Long-term biological
    adaptations, 53–56,
    57, 61
Lucy, 130–132
Lyell, Charles, 24, 26, 28,
    33–34, 37

M

Macaqes, 90
Macroevolution, 50–52
Madagascar, 66–67
Malthus, Thomas,
    30–31, 32
Martin, Robert, 117
Mayr, Ernst, 33–35, 38
Memories, 114–115
Mendel, Gregor, 40–44,
    47, 60
Mendelian genetics,
    40–44
Microevolution,
    47–48, 60
Miskawayh, Ibn, 20, 34
Missing link, 104
Modern evolutionary
    synthesis, 52
Molecular clocks, 74–76,
    126
Monkeys, 83. See also
    New World monkeys;
    Old World monkeys

Morotopithecus, 77
Mutations, 48–49,
    50, 61

N

Nails, 85
Natural selection, 14, 32,
    48, 49–50, 113
New World monkeys, 14,
    64, 67–68, 70, 97
Noah's ark, 22
Nurture, 50

O

Old World monkeys, 14,
    64, 67, 70, 97
Olduvai Gorge,
    123–124
Oligopithecus, 72
Omnivores, 84, 98
"One (adult) male
    group" social structure,
    93–94
Orangutans, 77, 93, 97,
    103
*Origin of Species by
    Means of Natural
    Selection, On the*
    (Darwin), 33, 38
Orrorin tugensis, 127,
    135

P

Paleoanthropology,
    defined, 13
Pan, 103, 136
*Paranthropus
    aethiopicus*, 133
Paranthropus boisei, 133
Paranthropus robustus,
    133
Park, Michael Alan, 13
Particulate factors,
    42, 60

Pea experiments,
    40–44, 60
Pelvises, 108–110
Phylogenies, 74–76, 104
Physiological
    incompatibility, 52
Pickford, Martin, 127
Pierolapithecus, 78
Plants, 54, 58–59
Platyrrhines, 67–68, 80
Plesiadapiformes, 64
Pliocene, hominins of,
    128–135
Ponginae, 103
Population genetics,
    47, 60
Populations, 48–49,
    50–52
Posture, primates and,
    84–86
Potato-washing, 96
Predators, 48, 91, 107
Primates
    behavioral traits of,
        94–95
    classification of,
        82–83
    diet and teeth of, 86
    emergence of hap-
        lorhines, ancestral
        humans and,
        68–78
    haplorhines, 65,
        67–68
    humans and, 97–98
    learning, tools and,
        96–97
    limbs, posture, loco-
        motion of, 84–86
    overview of, 64–66,
        83–84, 88–89,
        98–99
    reproduction, life
        cycle and, 88

    skull, brain, senses of,
        86–88
    social behavior of,
        89–94
    social structures of
        non-human, 92–94
    strepsirhines, 65,
        66–67
Primatology, 88–90
Principles of Geology
    (Lyell), 24
Proconsul, 73, 76–77, 102
Prosimians, 64, 65, 70, 80
Protection, social
    behaviors and, 91
Proteins, 45
Proteopithecus, 72
Punctuated equilibria,
    58, 61

R

Radioactive decay, 26
Rangwapithecus, 102
Ray, John, 20–21, 34, 37
Recessive traits, 42–44, 60
Redundancy, 115
Reproduction, primates
    and, 88

S

*Sahelanthropus
    tchadensis*, 126–127,
    135
Sarich, Vincent, 74–76
Savage-Rumbaugh, Sue,
    89
Schrödinger, Erwin, 19
Scientific names, 125
Seasonal isolation, 52
Sedimentary rocks, 22,
    123–124
Seed-bearing plants,
    58–59
Self-awareness, 113

Senses, primates and, 86–88
Senut, Brigitte, 127
Sexual dimorphism, 72–73
Short-term biological adaptations, 53–56, 57, 61
Siamangs, 93
Sign language, 89
"Single female and her offspring" social structure, 92–93
Sivapithecus, 77–78
Skulls, 86–88, 99, 107–108
Smell, 87
Smith, William, 24
Social behavior, 73, 89–94, 99, 113
Social grooming, 95
Social groups, 67
Somatic cells, 46–47
Species, defined, 51
Stanford, Craig, 68–69, 76, 117, 119
Stereoscopic vision, 67–68
Stratigraphy, 24

Strepsirhines, 65, 66–67, 70, 80
Systema Naturae (Linnaeus), 21

T

Taoism, 20
Taung child, 133
Taxonomy, 20–21
Technological adaptations, 54
Teeth, 86, 98, 110–112
Theories, 26, 28, 37
Theory of the Earth (Hutton), 23–24
Thermoregulation, 107
Thumbs, opposable, 84
Tibias, 110
Time, measurement of, 25–26, 74–76, 126
Tools, 96–97, 99
Toumai, 126–127
Trackways, 132
Transformation of species, 29
Transformism, 29
Transitional forms, 64
Transmutation of species, 29

Troop social structure, 94
Troops, 92

U

Uniformitarianism, 24, 37
Ussher, James, 22, 34

V

Vertebral columns, 107–108
Vertical clingers, 84
Vision, 67–68, 87–88, 99

W

Wallace, Alfred, 32–33, 34, 36, 37
Wilson, Allan, 74–76
Wolpoff, Milford, 105, 107, 115, 126–127

Y

Yerkes, Robert, 90

Z

Zhuangzi, 20, 34
Zoonomia (E. Darwin), 28

ABOUT THE AUTHOR

THOM HOLMES is a writer specializing in natural history subjects and dinosaurs. He is noted for his expertise on the early history of dinosaur science in America. He was the publications director of *The Dinosaur Society* for five years (1991–1997) and the editor of its newsletter, *Dino Times*, the world's only monthly publication devoted to news about dinosaur discoveries. It was through the Society and his work with the Academy of Natural Sciences in Philadelphia that Thom developed widespread contacts and working relationships with paleontologists and paleo-artists throughout the world.

Thom's published works include *Fossil Feud: The Rivalry of America's First Dinosaur Hunters* (Silver Burdett Press, September 1997); *The Dinosaur Library* (Enslow, *2001–2002*); *Duel of the Dinosaur Hunters* (Pearson Education, *2002*); *Fossil Feud: The First American Dinosaur Hunters* (Silver Burdett/Julian Messner, 1997). His many honors and awards include the National Science Teachers Association's *Outstanding Science Book of 1998,* VOYA's 1997 Nonfiction Honor List, an Orbis Pictus Honor, and the Chicago Public Library Association's *"Best of the Best"* in science books for young people.

Thom did undergraduate work in geology and studied paleontology through his role as a staff educator with the Academy of Natural Sciences in Philadelphia. He is a regular participant in field exploration, with two recent expeditions to Patagonia in association with Canadian, American, and Argentinian universities.